FATON BISLIMI

# NEWBORN KOSOVA:
## Some Development and Public Policy Challenges

Prishtina, Kosova / Houston, Texas, USA
June 2008

FATON BISLIMI

# NEWBORN KOSOVA:
## Some Development and Public Policy Challenges

Published jointly by:
*The Victory University College Press / Kolegji Universitar "Victory"*
Prishtina, Kosova
*Jalifat Publishing*
Houston, Texas, United States of America

Original Cover (2008 Edition) by:
Mithat Sejdiu
*www.pinguinistudio.com*

Layout and Design (2008, 2010 Editions):
*The Bislimi Group Foundation*
*www.bislimi.org*

\* \* \*

*This is a reprinted 2010 edition*

*"Success is how high you bounce when you hit bottom."*
General George Patton

4

This book is a collection of some academic papers that I wrote during my time in the MPAID program of the Kennedy School of Government, Harvard University. All of these papers have one thing in common—they directly or indirectly deal with some development and public policy (such as education, for instance) challenges that Kosova faces.

The quote from Gen. Patton is very much descriptive of Kosova's fate today—its success will be the height of its bounce after it hit the bottom. Kosova hit the bottom during the Kosova War of 1998-99. Now, after its declaration of independence of February 17, 2008, Kosova is in the process of bouncing. How high will it bounce will depend on many factors—some of which I explore in this book.

One technical note – I would like to bring to your attention the fact that these papers have not been modified since they were originally written. Even though written before Kosova's independence, the topics they deal with remain quite valid even today. You will notice that similar sections, such as that of a brief introduction and background of Kosova, will appear in most of them. This is because each of these papers was prepared individually and I wanted to keep them in their original form, despite the repetitions of the introduction and background sections. I hope, nevertheless, that this will cause you no inconvenience. I also decided to use the original spelling of the country name – Kosova, instead of the commonly used Kosovo, which comes from the Serbian version of it.

Finally, I would like to thank one of my best friends and a fellow MPAIDer, Ilker Ersegün Kayhan, who is also the co-author of one of the major pieces in this book. Furthermore, special thanks go to all of my Harvard Kennedy School professors. I very much appreciate the support of my family (my wife Nora, my parents Halit and Sefete, my sisters, Dafina and Drenusha) as well as my US host family (the Hinkhouses) during my time at Harvard.

I hope this book will spur up a constructive debate on these challenges that Kosova faces so that the best possible solutions are achieved. Enjoy reading.

Faton H. Bislimi
Prishtina, Kosova
May 2008

# Introduction

*The problems and issues explored in this book are quite important for determining the future paths of Kosovo. Development does not happen on its own. Development requires particular attention to all the problems hindering it. Therefore, exploring such problems is a good first step, especially when considering the fact that no problem can be solved unless it is well defined.*

*Kosovo stands today at a very crucial crossroad. It may start developing – both economically and socially – and become a sustainable and prosperous country. Or it may stagnate further, which can only bring more economic and social depression, both of which are terribly destabilizing factors.*

*By exploring several development challenges and issues – such as the effects of remittances on their recipients in Kosovo, for instance – Faton "Tony" Bislimi has provided significant insights for development practitioners and policymakers who care about Kosovo's future.*

*Overall, Bislimi's work, as a young development economist, is one of the first in-depth studies of this nature that provides not only good explorations of problems, but it also gets into some policy recommendations that may help resolve the problems at hand.*

*I trust this book can serve as a good foundation for a constructive debate on these important issues for Kosovo.*

**Frode Mauring**
**UNDP Resident Representative and UN Development Coordinator**
United Nations Development Programme
Prishtina, Kosovo

**Contents:**

# THE SPOIL EFFECT

# How Remittances Affect Developing Countries:

# The Case of Kosova

*Faton Bislimi & Ersegün Kayhan*[1]

[1] This is Faton (Tony) Bislimi and Ilker Ersegün Kayhan's Second-Year Policy Analysis (master thesis) for their Kennedy School of Government, Harvard University MPAID degrees, March 2007.

# THE SPOIL EFFECT

## *How Remittances Affect Developing Countries: The Case of Kosova*

**Acknowledgements:** *We would like to thank Professors Federico Sturzenegger, Joseph Stern, and Michael Walton for their advice, support, and guidance during our SYPA work. Also, we would like to thank Mr. Halit Bislimi of the The Bislimi Group Education for Peace Scholarships Program in Prishtina for the technical and logistical support, and Mr. Joseph DioGuardi and Mrs. Shirley Cloyes DioGuardi of the Albanian American Foundation for the financial support of Tony's field work in Kosova during the summer 2006.*

## Executive Summary

Remittances present one of the major sources of income for poor and developing countries. So far the literature on remittances has mainly been focused on comparative studies at the macro level, with a very few studies shedding light on the microeconomic effects.

This study focuses on the microeconomic effects of remittances on individual recipients in Kosova. Our initial hypothesis posits that besides their positive effects, remittances are also associated with negative effects — especially as far as education attainment and labor force participation of remittance recipients go. We believe that remittances create a form of reluctance towards education attainment and labor force participation on the recipients. We call this phenomenon the Spoil Effect.

To prove our theory, we use the World Bank's 2000 Living Standard Measurement Survey data on Kosova for our empirical analysis. Through simple OLS regressions, we establish strong negative correlations between remittances and education attainment and labor force participation. To tackle the issue of reverse causality and omitted variable bias, we use instrumental variables. Our Two-Stage Least Squares regressions using remittance instrumental variables reinforce our results and prove the existence of the spoil effect.

The existence of the spoil effect presents a major problem in the case of Kosova, which is heavily dependent on remittances. The longer the spoil effect persists, the more Kosovars will be without adequate education attainment and work experience. A poorly educated and unskilled workforce for a poor country like Kosova is no help for development.

Therefore, the Kosova policymakers are to seriously tackle this issue. To try to minimize the spoil effect, among other things, we highly recommend that the Kosova government should work on developing a policy that facilitates a Purpose Specific Payment System for Kosova migrants who want to support their family members or relatives in Kosova to attain higher education levels, for instance. This kind of system would help the migrants make sure that their remittances are being used for specific purposes (like education, healthcare, etc.) rather than to contribute to the spoil effect (by making the recipients indolent).

## 1. Introduction

Worker remittances sent from people working abroad to their families in their home country form an important source of income in many developing countries.[2] The ways in which the recipients utilize remittances vary: they can be used to cover daily expenses;

---

2 Financial and Private Sector Development – Remittances, World Bank, 2007

they can provide a cushion against emergencies, or rarely, people can use those funds to make small investments.

In this paper, we will briefly review some key questions on the impact of remittances on development and how this income inflow can be channeled to positively affect development. Furthermore, we will focus our study on Kosova and will consider any potential policy recommendations, which could be regarded as helpful in the process of designing better development strategies taking into account the effects of remittances.

More importantly, our key question is whether there may be a negative impact of remittances on development. One potential negative impact of remittances on development may be, what we call, the "Spoil Effect." Our initial hypothesis is that remittances may encourage the recipients to become indolent and "spoiled," particularly towards working and education attainment. Thus, labor force participation and level of education of the remittance-recipient household members may be negatively correlated with remittances they receive. To put it in another way, the Spoil Effect may be creating reluctance towards education attainment and working for remittance recipients.

As noted by a World Bank study, remittances are an important source of external finance for developing countries. They are second only to foreign direct investment as a source of external finance. One other important point is that remittances may even be counter-cyclical in times of economic recession. Additionally, remittances are well targeted to the needs of the recipients, who are usually struggling against poverty, because the persons sending the remittances know the recipients well. They can also be altruistic transfers that do not have to be paid back, which is very favorable for the balance of payments of the recipient country.[3]

Regarding the effect of remittances on development, according to this World Bank study, assuming that the poor migrate and send back remittances, remittances are believed to reduce poverty. However, this may not always be the case.

Moreover, it is also argued that remittances may increase inequality, because it can be the rich (more able) who migrate and send back remittances, making recipients even richer.[4] At the macro level this question can be studied using cross-country data, and at the micro level

---

[3] Dilip Ratha, "Understanding the Importance of Remittances," World Bank, October 1, 2004

[4] ibid.

17

using household surveys. Nevertheless, the impact of remittances depends on their use, like on schooling of children, pure consumption, small investments, savings, etc.

As for this paper, it is organized in the following manner: in the next section, we will give a brief overview of remittances from an international perspective, paying some particular attention to their volume and their rate of growth over time. In Section III, the economic effects of remittances are briefly discussed. Section IV describes the case of Kosova, which is a country 'exporting' a sizable portion of its population to the West. In Section V, we describe the meaning of "Spoil Effect," explain the data and the household survey that we used in this study, present our empirical analysis and the results pertaining to the existence of the "Spoil Effect" in Kosova. Section VI presents our conclusions and policy recommendations.

## 2. Overview – An International Perspective

The total volume of worker remittances worldwide is huge and the officially recorded remittance flows have also been increasing rapidly over the past years. Additionally, to explain how much more the remittances might have been increasing worldwide, it is also worthwhile to mention that the estimates and figures derived from the officially recorded remittance estimates may significantly underestimate the real magnitudes of remittances, as there is a large volume of informal flows. According to the World Bank, household surveys suggest that informal flows could add at least 50 percent to the official estimate.[5] There can also be a significant amount of error in formal figures due to the under-recording of flows or misclassification of remittances as export revenue, tourism receipts or non-resident deposits.

According to the World Bank estimates of the true size of remittances — that is with informal flows included — the total value worldwide was over $230 billion in 2005, involving around 175 million migrants. For some countries, remittances are voluminous. As a striking example, the champion in Latin America is Mexico receiving $20 billion of remittances in 2005 according to the Inter American Development Bank.[6] To have a broad idea about how workers' remittances to developing

---

[5] *Global Economic Prospects*, World Bank, 2006
[6] ibid.

countries have increased, it is worthwhile to take a glance at the following table.

**Table 2.1: Workers' Remittances to Developing Countries, 1990-2005**

| USD Billions | 1990 | 1995 | 2000 | 2001 | 2002 | 2003 | 2004e | 2005e | Change (%) 2005-2001 |
|---|---|---|---|---|---|---|---|---|---|
| Developing Countries | 31.2 | 57.8 | 85.6 | 96.5 | 113.4 | 142.1 | 160.4 | 166.9 | 73.0 |
| Lower Middle income | 13.9 | 30.0 | 42.6 | 47.4 | 57.3 | 72.5 | 83.5 | 88.0 | 86.0 |
| Upper Middle Income | 9.1 | 14.5 | 20.0 | 22.3 | 23.0 | 27.8 | 33.0 | 33.8 | 52.0 |
| Low Income | 8.1 | 13.3 | 22.8 | 26.8 | 33.1 | 41.8 | 43.9 | 45.0 | 68.0 |
| Latin Am & Caribbean | 5.8 | 13.4 | 20.1 | 24.4 | 28.1 | 34.8 | 40.7 | 42.4 | 74.0 |
| South Asia | 5.6 | 10.0 | 17.2 | 19.2 | 24.2 | 31.1 | 31.4 | 32.0 | 67.0 |
| East Asia & Pacific | 3.3 | 9.7 | 16.7 | 20.1 | 27.2 | 35.8 | 40.9 | 43.1 | 114.0 |
| Middle East & North Afr | 11.4 | 13.4 | 13.2 | 15.1 | 15.6 | 18.6 | 20.3 | 21.3 | 41.0 |
| Europe & Central Asia | 3.2 | 8.1 | 13.4 | 13.0 | 13.3 | 15.1 | 19.4 | 19.9 | 53.0 |
| Sub-Saharan Africa | 1.9 | 3.2 | 4.9 | 4.7 | 5.2 | 6.8 | 7.7 | 8.1 | 72.0 |
| World (Dev'ing & Industrl) | 68.6 | 101.6 | 131.5 | 147.1 | 166.2 | 200.2 | 225.8 | 232.3 | 58.0 |

*Source:* Global Development Prospects, World Bank (2006)

Additionally, remittances now account for almost one third of total global external finance. Moreover, according to the World Bank, the flow of remittances seems to be significantly more stable than that of other forms of external finance. To better understand the importance of remittances as a source of foreign exchange, the World Bank is directly quoted as saying: "Recorded remittance receipts were equivalent to about 6.7 percent of developing countries' imports and 7.5 percent of domestic investment. They also were larger than official flows and private equity (non-FDI) flows in 2004. Remittances were larger than public and private capital inflows in 36 developing countries in 2004 and larger than total merchandise exports in Albania, Bosnia and Herzegovina, Cape Verde, Gaza, Haiti, Jamaica, Kiribati, Lebanon, Nepal, Samoa, Serbia and Montenegro, and Tonga. In another 28 countries, they were larger than the earnings from the most important commodity export; for example, in Mexico, remittances are larger than FDI; in Sri Lanka, they are larger than tea exports; and in Morocco, they are larger than tourism receipts."[7]

The remittances as a share of GDP for low-income countries as of 2004 were 3.7% of their GDP, while for high-income OECD countries they were 0.2% of their GDP.[8] This means that for low-income countries, remittances are a more important external financing source than for the high-income countries. As can be seen from Fig. 2.1, the remittances as a share to GDP can be as high as 30% of GDP for low-income countries. Let us state the position of Kosova in this midst: remittances as a share of GDP were 15.07% as of 2005.[9]

[7] *Global Economic Prospects*, World Bank, 2006, page 88.
[8] *Balance of Payments Yearbook 2004*, IMF, 2004
[9] *BPK Annual Report 2005*, Banking and Payment Authority of Kosova, May 2006

**Figure 2.2: Top Twenty Remittance-Recipient Countries as Share of GDP**

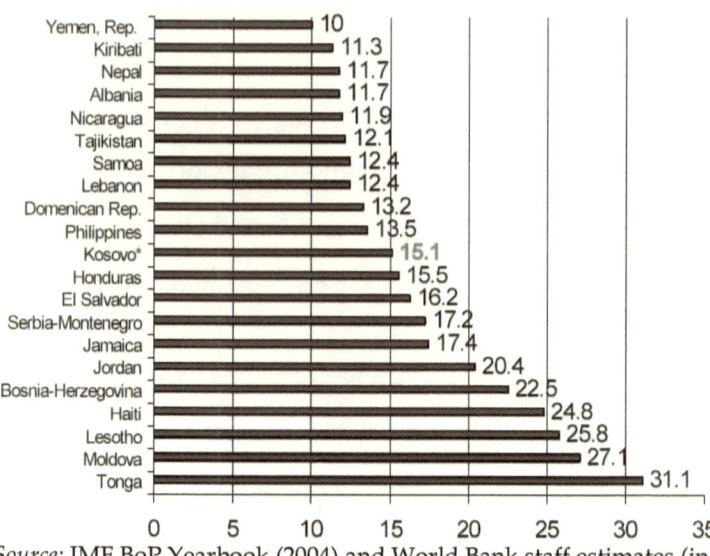

*Source:* IMF BoP Yearbook (2004) and World Bank staff estimates (in GEP 2006)

\* Position of Kosova in this ranking was added by authors

# 3. Economic Effects of Remittances

## 3.1. *Effects of Remittances on Poverty and Inequality*

There are indirect effects of remittances on income through their effects on growth, inflation, and exchange rates. However, the more easily observable and measurable effect of remittances is direct, since it affects poverty by increasing the income of the recipient.

22

According to the World Bank, there are a few ways to measure the effect of remittances on poverty: poverty simulation models, which asks the question 'how would poverty rates of the countries change if the remittances disappear completely?' or cross-country regressions. It is not easy to run cross-country regressions to study the effect of remittances on poverty, because it requires household data and most available household surveys do not have usable data on remittances.

The World Bank staff runs a simple poverty simulation model using cross-country data for 81 countries.[10] According to the results, the impact of remittances disappearing depends on their initial level, and the initial level of poverty. For instance, the World Bank found the average increase in the poverty headcount ratio for higher remittance countries (12.2 percentage points) is more than double that of the lower-remittance countries (5.0 percentage points).[11] Moreover, the impact is greater for those countries with higher headcount ratios to start with (Table 3. 1. 1). These results indicate the remittances play a role in poverty reduction, but the

[10] *Global Economic Prospects*, World Bank, 2006
[11] ibid.

results are not conclusive because of the simplicity of the model.

**Table 3. 1. 1: Simulated Impact of Eliminating Remittances on Poverty Rate**

| Country Group | No. of Countries | Remittances/GDP (%) | Poverty Headcount Rate | Poverty Headcount Rate, no Gini change |
|---|---|---|---|---|
| Low Remittances | 23 | 2.2 | 25.6 | 5.0 |
| Low Headcount Rate | 12 | 2.0 | 11.8 | 1.2 |
| High Headcount Rate | 11 | 2.5 | 40.6 | 9.1 |
| High Remittances | 14 | 11.0 | 24.8 | 12.2 |
| Low Headcount Rate | 7 | 8.0 | 10.7 | 4.1 |
| High Headcount Rate | 7 | 14.1 | 38.9 | 20.3 |

*Source:* GEP, World Bank (2006)

In the economics literature related to remittances, there are more rigorous studies that try to establish the link between remittances and poverty levels based on cross-country data. A study of 71 developing countries showed that a 10 percent increase in per capita official international remittances led to a 3.5 percent decline in the share of people living in poverty.[12] There are other recent studies that have confirmed these findings: IMF uses a sample of 101 countries for the period of 1970-2003, and reaches very similar results.[13] To sum up, the evidence presented in the literature suggests that remittances do reduce poverty.

---

[12] Adams, Richard and John Page, "Do International Migration and Remittances Reduce Poverty in Developing Countries?" *World Development* 33(10): 1645–69, 2005

[13] *World Economic Outlook*, IMF, 2005

On the other hand, regarding the effect of remittances on inequality, there are no strong conclusions found yet in household studies of the relationship between remittances and inequality. World Bank staff states: "remittances sometimes go disproportionately to better-off households and so widen disparities, but in other cases they appear to target the less well off, causing disparities to shrink."[14] Income disparities, however, are not of concern in this study.

### 3.2. Effects of Remittances on Household Consumption Smoothing

Poor households lacking access to proper insurance and credit markets are particularly vulnerable to adverse shocks, and according to the World Bank, remittances can play a significant role in consumption smoothing.[15] One strategy of households to reduce risk, however, is to send the family members to other regions or abroad, where the same income shock is not likely to occur. A very interesting example of this comes from a study in India. The more volatile a household's income, the further away such households in rural India tend to

---

[14] *Global Economic Prospects*, World Bank, 2006
[15] ibid.

send their daughters to marry. Their purpose is to insure the household against risks.[16] Another example of a favorable effect of remittances on consumption smoothing comes from a study on Botswana. Remittances to Botswana increased as the drought in the migrant's home region increased.[17] For the case of Kosova, our data shows that the expenditure of the household is positively correlated with the remittance amount it receives.[18]

Although studies on the effects of remittances on consumption smoothing support the view that remittances provide some insurance, interpreting the correlations is complicated. There is always the likelihood of reverse causality (remittances can be as well affected by the household income as they affect the household income). And, there is always the question of omitted variable bias.[19]

## 3.3. Effects of Remittances on Labor Supply

As stated in the introduction, labor supply is a major focus of our study. There is evidence in the literature indicating

---

[16] Rosenzweig, Mark R., and Oden Stark, "Consumption Smoothing, Migration, and Marriage: Evidence from Rural India." *Journal of Political Economy* 97(4): 906–26, 1989

[17] Lucas, Robert, and Oded Stark, "Motivations to Remit: Evidence from Botswana" *Journal of Political Economy* 93: 901–18, 1985

[18] See Appendix A for regression results

[19] *Global Economic Prospects*, World Bank, 2006

that remittances may tend to reduce the labor supply of the remaining household members (through an income substitution effect). For example, a rise in remittances decreased labor force participation in Managua, Nicaragua, while at the same time increasing self-employment.[20] In a number of Caribbean countries, remittances were estimated to reduce the participation rates of remaining household members, but the direction of causality was hard to establish.[21] In another study on Mexico, using the sample of rural households in Mexico in 2000, which vary according to whether they have sent migrants to the US or received remittances from the US, it was found that remaining household members were less likely to participate in the labor force if their households have either sent migrants to the US or received remittances from the US, controlling for observable characteristics.[22]

On the other hand, other studies and research have shown that remittances have also proven to reduce the

---

[20] Funkhouser, Edward, "Migration from Nicaragua: Some Recent Evidence." *World Development* 20(3): 1209–18, 1992

[21] Itzigsohn, Jose, "Migrant Remittances, Labor Markets, and Household Strategies: A Comparative Analysis of Low-Income Household Strategies in the Caribbean Basin" *Social Forces*, 74(2):633-655, 1995

[22] Hanson, Gordon H., "Emigration, Remittances, and Labor Force Participation in Mexico," IADB, 2006

supply of child labor, and to increase the supply of adult labor, as is the case with the Philippines, for instance.[23]

## 3.4. Effects of Remittances on Savings and Investments

If used for small investments, remittances can be instrumental in providing working capital to the entrepreneurs remaining in the home country. They can also have multiplier effects. For example, one dollar sent from the Mexican workers in the US back to their hometown was estimated to boost Mexico's GDP by $2.90.[24]

Remittances can lead to investments in education and health. For example, in a study on El Salvador, remittances were estimated to reduce the probability of children leaving school by a factor of ten as compared to the impact of other sources of income in urban areas, and by 2.6 times in rural areas.[25] Cox and Ureta, in that study,

[23] Yang, Dean, "International Migration, Human Capital, and Entrepreneurship: Evidence from Philippine Migrant's Exchange Rate Shocks," Research Program on International Migration and Development, DECRG, Policy Research Working Paper 3578, World Bank, 2004

[24] Adelman, I., and J. E. Taylor, "Is Structural Adjustment with a Human Face Possible?" *Journal of Development Studies* 26: 387–407, 1992

[25] Cox Edwards, Alejandro, and Manuelita Ureta, "International Migration, Remittances, and Schooling: Evidence from El Salvador." *Journal of Development Economics* 72(2): 429–61, 2003

say that the reason why remittances had a disproportionate effect on schooling was because the migrants made school attendance a condition for financial support. However, remittances can also encourage entrepreneurship. A 2003 survey of 6,000 small firms in 44 urban areas in Mexico showed that almost 20 percent of the total capital in urban micro enterprises was derived from remittances.[26]

Some recent work in this field estimates that remittances are also mostly saved and invested. For instance, in Egypt, the remittances were used largely to invest in housing construction and in the acquisition of agricultural or commercial land.[27] Very similar results were later found in a study on Pakistan.[28] In an even later study of Guatemala, the households that received remittances were found to have lower marginal propensities to consume and a higher propensity to invest in education, health, and housing than households

[26] Woodruff, Christopher, and Rene Zenteno, "Remittances and Microenterprises in Mexico," *Graduate School of International Relations and Pacific Studies*, University of California–San Diego, 2001

[27] Adams, Richard, "The Economic Uses and Impact of International Remittances in Rural Egypt," *Economic Development and Cultural Change* 39(4): 695–722, 1991

[28] Adams, Richard, "Remittances, Investment, and Rural Asset Accumulation in Pakistan," *Economic Development and Cultural Change* 41(1): 155–73, 1998

receiving no remittances.[29] As for the case of Kosova, it is hard to claim with accuracy whether remittances have been used mainly for a particular purpose. We know, however, that education is one of the smaller non-food household monthly expenditures (constituting only 2.80% of the total non-food expenditures, which is 24.31% of total household expenditure).[30]

## 4. The Case of Kosova

### 4.1. A Brief Historical and Economic Background

Kosova, an equally constituent part of the Yugoslavian Federation, was illegally and unwillingly stripped of its autonomous and constituent status within the Federation in 1989 by Belgrade, and as a result became one of the poorest and least developed parts of Yugoslavia, and even Europe. The decade of the 1990s marked a remarkable civil resistance of ethnic Albanians,

---

[29] Adams, Richard, "Remittances, Household Expenditure and Investment in Guatemala," in *International Migration, Remittances, and the Brain Drain*, ed. Caglar Ozden and Maurice Schiff, World Bank, 2005

[30] *Private Income in Kosova 2003-2005*, Statistical Office of Kosova, Prishtina, September 2006

who constitute over 90 % of Kosova's two million people, against the Serbian apartheid.

But, this civil resistance and the belief that the civilized world would come to support Kosova Albanians in their quest for freedom started to fade in the late 1990s. By 1997 armed guerilla Albanian groups emerged. The support for the armed resistance took a steep increase in 1998 when the Kosova Liberation Army (KLA) became publicly and officially the armed movement of Kosova Albanians fighting for freedom. The emergence of KLA triggered the Serb forces to undertake massive military offensives throughout Kosova during late 1998 and early 1999, resulting in mass murders and brutal expulsions. Such a grand-scale ethnic cleansing in the heart of Europe could no longer be  tolerated, bringing about NATO's intervention.

Until NATO's first war in the history of its existence, very few people knew where Kosova was or anything else about it.  However, scenes of brutality and genocide committed by Serbian forces against the ethnic Albanian civilian population of Kosova shook the world in early 1999 and made Kosova a violently radiant place on the world map. To stop this unfolding "New Holocaust" — as many personalities familiar with the history of the

Balkans and that of Kosova have put it—NATO engaged in a 79-day air strike campaign against Serbian forces.

Since NATO's successful military intervention, which resulted in all Serbian forces being withdrawn from Kosova, the country was put under the United Nations administration. According to the UNSC Resolution 1244 of 10 June 1999, the UN Mission in Kosova (UNMIK) was called upon to:[31]

- perform basic civilian administrative functions;
- promote the establishment of substantial autonomy and self-government in Kosova;
- facilitate a political process to determine Kosova's future status;
- coordinate humanitarian and disaster relief of all international agencies;
- support the reconstruction of key infrastructure;
- maintain civil law and order;
- promote human rights; and
- assure the safe and unimpeded return of all refugees and displaced persons to their homes in Kosova.

---

[31] United Nations Mission in Kosova (official web-page)

However, UNMIK was neither mandated, nor sufficiently capable to assist Kosova in its much needed development effort. That is a task that was left to the European Union.

But, Kosova's economy was not only underdeveloped to begin with; it had also been harshly damaged for over a decade during the Serbian rule. As also noted by IMF, "the war provided a further setback to output and the quality and capacity of the infrastructure. Damage to the housing stock was particularly extensive, but the main utilities (power, telecommunications) also suffered considerable damage, as did some of the already dubiously viable industrial concerns."[32]

During the Serbian rule of the 1990s, Kosova Albanians were massively dismissed from public jobs. Being a socialist economy, most of the jobs in Kosova were in the public domain. So, this massive dismissal of Kosova Albanians created huge unemployment, which naturally fed into an increase in poverty. Being an Albanian in Kosova during the period of Serbian domination was an excuse not only to be dismissed from a job, but also to be

---

[32] Robert Corker, Dawn Rehm, Kristina Kostial, "Kosova: Macroeconomic Issues and Fiscal Sustainability," IMF 2001

denied any public services—some as essential as health care and education.

Nevertheless, Kosova Albanians managed to establish a parallel state run by a government-in-exile, which was successful in collecting voluntary, yet very significant amounts of money, into the Republic of Kosova Fund—named the "3 percent." This "3-percent" fund was mainly used to fund an underground education system and a quasi-public healthcare system. It also provided for a social welfare system to help those in extreme poverty.

Being a society with close family ties and very non-individualistic, Kosova Albanians in the diaspora played the most crucial role in ensuring the economic survival of the Albanians inside Kosova. Initially, only the diaspora members contributed into the "3-percent" fund. In addition, migrant Kosova Albanians, mainly residing in Western Europe, provided substantial financial assistance to their family, relatives, and friends in Kosova, especially over the decade of the 1990s.

## 4.2. Remittances—A Lifeline for Kosova Albanians

Historically, remittance inflows have been greater for the poorer countries. Kosova is no exception. As a matter of fact, Kosova might even be considered an outliner in remittance inflows. As stated above, Albanians in general are a "family first" kind of society. Family respect and moral, along with their trust (besa), are Albanians' core values dating back to their predecessors, ancient and autochthon rulers of the Balkans, the Illyrians.[33]

Modern literature distinguishes between three distinct waves of immigration of Albanians from Kosova:[34]

- the first one took place during the 1960s and 1970s when mainly unskilled people from rural Kosova immigrated primarily to Germany and Switzerland;

- the second one took place during the 1980s and 1990s when more educated and skilled people, mostly young, left Kosova in an attempt to avoid the mandatory Yugoslav military service during the Balkans wars; and

- the third one took place during the Kosova War of 1998-99 when almost one million Kosova Albanians were forcefully expulsed from their

[33] Shirley Cloyes DioGuardi, "Jewish Survival in Albania and the Ethics of 'Besa'", American Jewish Congress, Congress Monthly Jan/Feb 2006, NY.
[34] Barbara Balaj, "Kosova's Albanian Diaspora: Blessing or Curse on Economy?" *Beyond Transition*, Word Bank 2001

homes, creating a refugee catastrophe for neighboring Albania and Macedonia, to which the Western nations responded by airlifting thousands of these Kosova Albanians to countries in Western Europe and even the United States and Canada. Most of the Kosova Albanians that were taken to Western countries as refugees during the war have established and remained there permanently.

But, what we notice today is perhaps the fourth wave of immigration from Kosova. Due to lack of economic progress and high unemployment rate, many very skilled and highly educated Albanians are leaving Kosova on a daily basis, despite the difficulties in obtaining an entry visa for a Western country. A good portion of these individuals are also willing to pay as much as €10,000 ($13,320) to obtain a Western entry visa.[35] False or otherwise illegal visas have become quite a thriving market. For instance, the German Office in Prishtina was under investigation for visa issuance malpractice in early 2005.[36] Yet, the number of such

---

[35] "Demand Increases for Western Visas," *IliriaPost*, Prishtina, June 29, 2006

[36] *Fischer Scandal: Foreign Minister About to Fall Over Visa Scandal*, KAS Germany Update No.23, Feb 2005

individuals has rapidly increased in the last couple of years.

Table 4.2.1: The Kosova Albanian Diasporas

| Country | Number | Country | Number |
| --- | --- | --- | --- |
| Germany | 200,000 | Belgium | 8,000 |
| Switzerland | 155,000 | France | 5,000 |
| US/Canada | 55,000 | Denmark | 5,000 |
| Croatia | 40,000 | Italy | 4,000 |
| Sweden | 35,000 | Norway | 4,000 |
| Bosnia | 30,000 | UK | 2,500 |
| Albania | 25,000 | Netherlands | 2,000 |
| Austria | 23,000 | Finland | 600 |
| Slovenia | 15,000 | Luxembourg | 200 |
|  |  | Total: | **609,300** |

*Source:* The Demographic Department of Kosova (1995 estimates)

Even after the Kosova war was over quite a significant number of Kosova Albanians living in Western Europe have either voluntarily or by order of immigration authorities returned to Kosova, mainly from Germany. Nevertheless, the Kosova Albanian diaspora remains fairly large. More recent statistical estimates (2005) show that in Switzerland alone there are about 145,000 Kosova Albanians with legal residency status and some 50,000 asylum seekers in process.[37]

The Kosova Albanians working and living abroad continue to provide one of the major sources of income for Albanians living in Kosova. Given the very nature of

---

[37] Statistical Office of Kosova, Prishtina, 2005

remittances, it is obviously difficult to collect accurate data — hence, estimates are usually used. In the case of Kosova, various estimates have been produced.

According to the Banking and Payments Authority of Kosova, the average annual amount that Kosova receives in remittances was estimated to be about €568 million ($757 million).[38] On the other hand, estimates by the World Bank gave a slightly different figure averaging the annual remittance inflows to Kosova at about €550 million ($733 million). [39] Yet another set of estimates comes from IMF, as well, which shows the obvious discrepancies in remittance estimations.

Table: 4.2.2: Remittances and GDP in Kosova

| Year | Remittance Amount in € mil. | GDP in € mil. | Remittances as Percent of GDP |
|------|------|------|------|
| 2001 | 317 | 2,520 | 12.58% |
| 2002 | 341 | 2,447 | 13.94% |
| 2003 | 341 | 2,413 | 14.13% |
| 2004 | 339 | 2,501 | 13.55% |
| 2005 | 375 | 2,488 | 15.07% |
| 2006 | 347 | n/a | n/a |

*Source:* Remittance data from IMF Kosova Country Office (2006), and GDP data from Kosova Central Banking Authority (2006)

---

[38] *BPK Annual Report 2003*, Banking and Payments Authority of Kosova, Prishtina, March 2004

[39] *Kosova Economic Memorandum*, Report No: 28023-KOS, World Bank, Washington, 17 May 2004

Such inconsistencies and differences in remittance estimates reflect two major factors: first, remittances are sent through a variety of channels—both formal and informal; and second, the actual definition of remittances is unclear (do foreign pensions count as remittances?).

Until after the war and the establishment of a banking system in Kosova in late 1999, remittances have almost exclusively come into the country informally through persons carrying cash into Kosova from Western Europe.

---

**Box I: Bus Driver or Banker?**

"The bus driver was like our banker. My uncle would call one or two days in advance to tell us that the bus driver coming on this day to Gjilan would bring this amount of money for us. So, we would go and wait for the bus and meet with the driver after the passengers would leave to get the cash my uncle had sent from Hamburg. We have done this for years. Now, he usually sends money through the bank or Western Union."[40]

Gazmend Rrustemi, Student
Gjilan Kosova

---

With Kosova having established a fairly good banking system after the war, more migrant Kosova Albanians seem to be utilizing the bank and other money transfer institutions to send in their remittances. For

---

[40] Author's Personal Interview, Gjilan, Kosova, January 15, 2007

instance, Kasabank, one of the leading banks in Kosova processes about €24.6 million per month in international incoming transactions. Of this amount, about €212,000 are foreign pensions, and the bank estimates that some 30% are private remittances originating mostly in Germany, Austria, and Switzerland. Private remittances, while hard to estimate, average between €100 and €1,000 per individual transaction.[41]

The Central Banking Authority of Kosova (successor to the former Banking and Payments Authority of Kosova, as of August 2006), which will be Kosova's Central Bank once the country's political status is finally determined this year, estimates that remittances made up between 14 and 17 percent of Kosova's GDP over the period 2001-2006.[42]

The unemployment rate in Kosova has been unacceptably high. Even seven years after the war, unemployment remains at a staggering rate of about 40-60% (depending on the source.)[43]    Needless to say, remittances provide an important source of income for

---

[41] *Kasabank—Kosovar Remittances and Migrant Pensions*, Migrant Remittances, USAID and DFID E-Newsletter, Vol. 2, No. 2, August 2005

[42] *BPK Annual Report 2005*, Central Banking Authority of Kosova, Prishtina, May 2006

[43] Official statistics show unemployment at 39.7% (Statistical Office of Kosova, *Kosova in Figures 2005*), while many other articles and studies claim the rate of unemployment at about 60%.

quite a vast number of Kosovar households. About one out of ten households in Kosova depends on remittances.[44] More specifically, remittances constitute the second largest source of income for households in Kosova, after regular employment. In total, remittances (from family members and others abroad, including foreign pensions) make up about 16% of household income.[45]

**Table 4.2.3: Household Income Sources in Kosova (% of total income)**

| Income Source | Men | Women | All |
|---|---|---|---|
| Regular Wages | 51 | 58 | 51 |
| Temporary Wages | 7 | 1 | 6 |
| Business Net | 11 | 1 | 9 |
| Agriculture Net | 3 | 1 | 6 |
| From members abroad | 9 | 12 | 10 |
| From others abroad | 3 | 3 | 3 |
| Kosovo Pensions | 3 | 15 | 5 |
| Pensions from abroad | 3 | 2 | 3 |
| Remitt's from Kosovo | 1 | 1 | 1 |
| Property Income | 2 | 1 | 2 |
| Social Welfare | 2 | 3 | 3 |
| Lotteries | 0 | 0 | 0 |
| Other | 2 | 1 | 2 |
| Wages in kind | 1 | 1 | 1 |
| In kind from abroad | 0 | 0 | 0 |
| Total % | 100 | 100 | 100 |

*Source:* Statistical Office of Kosova (2006)

[44] *Private Income in Kosova 2003-2005*, Statistical Office of Kosova, Prishtina, September 2006
[45] *Private Income in Kosova 2003-2005*, Statistical Office of Kosova, Prishtina, September 2006

41

Despite its enormously high unemployment rate and its relatively small GDP and GDP per capita, in comparison to other countries in the region, Kosova's living standard along with the cost of living remain at about the same level with those of other countries in the region.[46]

**Figure 4.2.1: Western Balkans GDP year-on-year % changes**

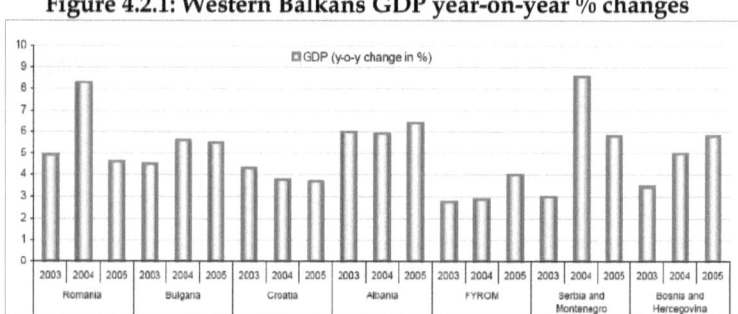

*Source:* Business Monitor International (2006), EBRD (2005) (in BPK Annual Report 2005)

**Figure 4.2.2: Kosova GDP growth (year-on-year) at constant 2002 prices**

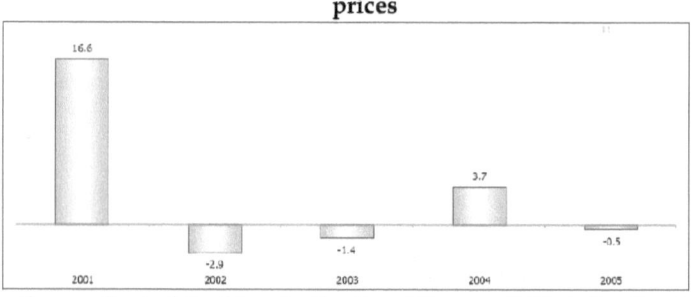

*Source:* Central Banking Authority of Kosova, IMF staff estimates (2005)

---

[46] *BPK Annual Report 2005*, Central Banking Authority of Kosova, Prishtina, May 2006

Nevertheless, given the significant amounts that Kosova receives in remittances from its migrant population, it is quite reasonable to question the effects they may have on Kosova's economic and social development.

## 5. The Spoil Effect
### 5.1. *Jobless, but Paid*

Remember the high unemployment rate in Kosova (between 40-60%)? Remember its relatively small GDP and its very vulnerable growth rate (as compared to the region—depicted in Figures 4.2.1 and 4.2.2 above)? Remember that over half of Kosova's population is of working age? Yet, Kosova remains a stable place. But, for how long this social stability will last is highly unpredictable.

Getting back to the focus of this study, let's reiterate that it is reasonable to assume that remittances (and foreign pensions to some extent) have dramatically helped by filling the obvious income gap for Kosova

Albanians. Some argue that cutting remittances will have a tremendously negative effect on Kosova.[47]

An eventual decrease in remittance inflows to Kosova, however, may happen due to several reasons. First, after the end of the Kosova war, the number of Kosova Albanians in the diaspora (especially true for some Western European countries) has decreased. Second, most of the current diaspora communities are no longer comprised of single working men alone (who usually would be able to save more and as a result send more money home). Third, the group of early migrants have been increasingly joined by their own families and consequently are able to send less cash to extended families in Kosova. And, fourth, the extent of generosity may begin to weaken as compared to the pre-war period, as more migrants believe that now that Kosova is free there should be more opportunities for their kin to work and be self-sufficient.

As seen in the previous part, remittances constitute the second biggest source of income for households in Kosova. Statistics show that about fifteen percent of Kosova households—the average household size is about

---

[47] *"Cutting the Lifeline: Migration, Families and the Future of Kosova"*, European Stability Initiative, Berlin September 2006

7 members[48] — are almost exclusively dependent on remittances.[49]

But, besides filling in this obvious income gap, what other effects may remittances have on their recipients? Our theory posits that individuals receiving remittances or those living in a remittance-recipient family may be less likely to attain more years of schooling as compared to those receiving no remittances. Moreover, being a remittance recipient or living in a remittance-receiving family may also be correlated to a person being less motivated to working and earning. Therefore, we suppose that remittances may be correlated to the existence of a reluctance in people as far as education and working are concerned — hence, the Spoil Effect.

---

**Box 2: The Spoil Effect**
One of the effects that remittances may have on their recipients could be the emergence of reluctance towards education and labor participation within these individuals. Such an effect is called the spoil effect.

---

Kosova is a dazzling place during the summer. Restaurants are usually packed, and so are the countless street cafés. Part of the reason for this booming activity is

---

[48] Kosova households are the largest in Europe.
[49] *"Cutting the Lifeline: Migration, Families and the Future of Kosova"*, European Stability Initiative, Berlin September 2006

that tens of thousands of Kosova Albanians living abroad visit Kosova over the summer. The same scenario is valid for winter holidays. The Prishtina International Airport, the only civil airport connecting Kosova to the rest of the world, is served by 14 international air carriers and serves about one million passengers per year—making it the busiest airport in the Western Balkans.[50]

However, not only when the diaspora visitors come, but also during other times of the year, restaurants and cafés around Kosova are usually packed, especially by young people. The paradox that inspired this study is obvious—Kosova youngsters are jobless, yet they seem to be able to afford spending money in cafés and restaurants, but not on education or professional training. The paradox becomes even more vivid when we compare household average monthly expenses with average monthly incomes.

**Table 5.1.1: Average Monthly Income for Households in Kosova (in €, June 2003-May 2004)**

[50] Prishtina International Airport - PRN (official web-page)
46

| Type of income | Residence | | Kosovo | Participation |
| | Urban | Rural | | (%) |
|---|---|---|---|---|
| Net wages & taxed salaries | 207.6 | 125.9 | 151.5 | 55.2 |
| Pensions | 13.6 | 21.2 | 18.8 | 6.8 |
| Social welfare benefits | 5.8 | 7.7 | 7.1 | 2.6 |
| Type of payment | 1.6 | 3.7 | 3.1 | 1.1 |
| Rent, dividends, interests | 5.8 | 0.6 | 2.2 | 0.8 |
| Cash remittance from Kosovo | 3.1 | 2.1 | 2.4 | 0.9 |
| Cash remittance from abroad | 25.0 | 41.7 | 36.4 | 13.3 |
| Net inc from private business in Kosovo | 33.8 | 19.8 | 24.2 | 8.8 |
| Presents sent to Kosovo from diaspora | 1.1 | 1.2 | 1.1 | 0.4 |
| Lotteries | 0.1 | 0.0 | 0.0 | 0.0 |
| Other income | 21.6 | 30.0 | 27.4 | 10.0 |
| Total | 319.1 | 253.9 | 274.3 | 100.0 |

*Source:* Statistical Office of Kosova (2006)

**Table 5.1.2: Average Monthly Expenditure of Households in Kosova (in €, June 2003-May 2004)**

| Type of Expenditure | Residence | | Kosovo | Participation |
| | Urban | Rural | | (%) |
|---|---|---|---|---|
| Food expenditure | 194.2 | 155.1 | 167.4 | 59.6 |
| Bread & cereals | 38.3 | 33.6 | 35.0 | 12.5 |
| Meat | 31.8 | 24.3 | 26.7 | 9.5 |
| Fish | 2.1 | 1.2 | 1.5 | 0.5 |
| Milk, cheese, eggs | 30.6 | 11.3 | 17.3 | 6.2 |
| Oil & fat | 8.0 | 8.6 | 8.4 | 3.0 |
| Fruits | 11.6 | 7.7 | 9.0 | 3.2 |
| Vegetables | 22.5 | 19.1 | 20.1 | 7.2 |
| Sugar, jam, honey | 9.8 | 10.9 | 10.5 | 3.8 |
| Other food products | 8.3 | 9.8 | 9.4 | 3.3 |
| Coffee, tea, cacao | 6.4 | 7.4 | 7.1 | 2.5 |
| Sweet drinks | 11.9 | 7.8 | 9.1 | 3.2 |
| Alcoholic beverages | 1.3 | 1.5 | 1.4 | 0.5 |
| Tobacco | 11.8 | 12.1 | 12.0 | 4.3 |
| Non-Food Products | 75.3 | 65.1 | 68.3 | 24.3 |
| Clothing | 11.0 | 13.7 | 12.8 | 4.6 |
| Footwear | 7.7 | 9.5 | 8.9 | 3.2 |
| Housing, related services | 35.2 | 20.6 | 25.2 | 9.0 |
| Household equipment | 13.2 | 13.9 | 13.7 | 4.9 |
| Household appliances | 8.2 | 7.5 | 7.7 | 2.7 |
| Telecommunication exp. | 27.0 | 23.3 | 24.4 | 8.7 |
| Culture and recreation exp. | 5.5 | 2.6 | 3.5 | 1.3 |
| School & education exp. | 7.9 | 7.9 | 7.9 | 2.8 |
| Hotel expenditure | 6.2 | 2.6 | 3.7 | 1.3 |
| Exp. On other goods & services | 7.0 | 5.2 | 5.8 | 2.1 |
| Total expenditures | 322.9 | 261.8 | 281.0 | 100.0 |

*Source:* Statistical Office of Kosova (2006)

Households in Kosova (both rural and urban ones) somehow manage to spend slightly more than their total income (see Tables 5.1.1 and 5.1.2). This "mysterious extra" money that they spend over their total accounted for income constitutes what we call "visit remittances." These are cash remittances provided to Kosova Albanians in Kosova during the visits of their migrant family or relatives. They are not accounted for as income or transfers because of their usual small size and informality of transfer.

A survey of 2,483 individuals[51] enjoying outdoor refreshments in cafés from three major towns in Kosova suggested that roughly half of the respondents receive remittances or live in a household that receives remittances from a family member abroad, while only about 40% have jobs and 52% have a family member abroad.

---

**Box 3: I don't have a job, but I have money**
"I started attending university in 2001, majoring in computer science. My uncle who lives in Switzerland has financially supported my education. After finishing two years of university studies, I kind of gave up. I was spending too much money and did not feel that once I graduate I could have a good job. My uncle still sends me money. He knows I

---

am technically still a student. And, I guess that's why I don't either look for a job. You know, if I worked, I could not make more than what I get from my uncle anyways. So far, so good… until the economy develops or until I can go abroad."[52]

V. B., Student
Gjilan, Kosova

**Table 5.1.3: Kosova Youngsters (of working age) Enjoying Cafés**

| City | No. of Respondents | employed | | has a family member abroad | | receive remittances | | male | | female | |
|------|------|------|------|------|------|------|------|------|------|------|------|
| Prishtina | 842 | 431 | 51% | 418 | 50% | 376 | 45% | 501 | 60% | 341 | 40% |
| Gjilan | 845 | 348 | 41% | 547 | 65% | 531 | 63% | 493 | 58% | 352 | 42% |
| Skenderaj | 796 | 218 | 27% | 334 | 42% | 326 | 41% | 618 | 78% | 178 | 22% |
| Total: | 2483 | 997 | 40% | 1299 | 52% | 1233 | 50% | 1612 | 65% | 871 | 35% |

*Source*: Author's survey (2006)

Moreover, as Table 5.1.3 shows, only about 18% of the respondents in cafés were both unemployed and not receiving remittances.

The phenomenon of the spoil effect is mostly seen in young people who spend considerable amounts of time—and even money—in places of relaxation and recreation, such as popular Kosova street-side café shops, instead of attending school or working (or at least looking for a job).

---

[52] Author's personal interview, Gjilan, Kosova, January 15, 2007

## 5.2. Education and Labor Force Participation

As per our definition of the spoil effect, we focus on two major pillars: education and labor participation. There are some significant studies that show education increases earnings, but whether it increases the level of development for a country remains unclear.[53] In the case of Kosova, given its small size, education is seen as a key to developing a competitive workforce, which could move Kosova closer to the global job market, [54] and eventually lead to some level of growth and development. As for labor participation, Kosova's economy is small and mainly agricultural—and Kosova has the youngest population in Europe with about 36,000 new people entering the labor market annually (Kosova has a workforce of about 924,000 and a population of about 2 million).[55]

As we look at Kosova's income sources by level of education, we see that remittances constitute some 25% of income for individuals with primary school, while only

---

[53] Esther Duflo, "Schooling and Labor Market Consequences of School Construction in Indonesia: Evidence from an Unusual Policy," *American Economic Review* 91(4), September 2001

[54] Faton Bislimi and Rob Gulick, "Building a Competitive Workforce in Kosova", American Chamber of Commerce in Kosova, Prishtina, Kosova, June 2005

[55] John Bradley and Gerald Knaus, "Towards a Development Plan for Kosova," ESPIG Policy Paper No. 1, Prishtina, Kosova, August 2004

3% of those with higher education. This could indicate that the more educated you are, the less likely you will be to receive remittances—or perhaps the more remittances you receive, the less likely you are to get more education, hence, the spoil effect. Notwithstanding the reverse causality issue (which we will tackle later), we believe the latter is true.

**Table 5.2.1: Income Source by Highest Education Level**

| Income Source | Primary | Secondary | Higher |
|---|---|---|---|
| Regular wages | 21% | 60% | 83% |
| Temporary wages | 9% | 6% | 1% |
| Business net | 4% | 15% | 6% |
| Agriculture net | 8% | 0% | 0% |
| Kosova pensions | 14% | 1% | 2% |
| Pensions from abroad | 7% | 1% | 1% |
| Social welfare | 5% | 2% | 0% |
| Remittances from abroad | 25% | 8% | 3% |
| Other | 6% | 6% | 4% |

*Source:* Statistical Office of Kosova (2006)

**Figure 5.2.1: Average Annual Income by Categories (in €)**

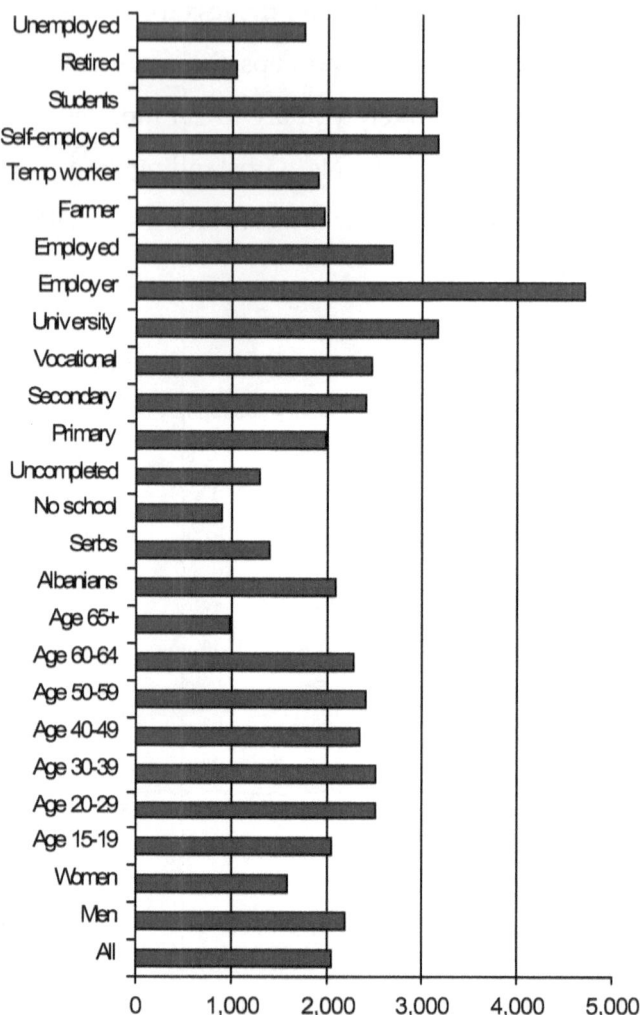

*Source*: Statistical Office of Kosova (2006)

Furthermore, as we look at the average annual income for different categories of the Kosova population, we notice yet another important indicator. Students constitute the second highest annual income group. Unemployed also range right in the mean annual income group. Naturally, one would raise the following questions: Why is a student making as much as a university educated professional? Why do the unemployed make almost as much as the mean income of the working population?

Moreover, why would a student finish his university education (or attain more years of education) when he is now making (mainly through remittances) as much as he would make with a university degree? Also, why would an unemployed person (usually receiving remittances) actively seek employment when the income he would earn is only slightly over what he makes now, and as a result he might lose the remittances he receives now? Both of these factors are important and feed right into the existence of our spoil effect.

As we turn to labor statistics, we find that over half of Kosova's population is of working age (15-64 years).[56] Yet, the unemployment rate remains very high,

---

[56] *Kosova in Figures 2005,* Statistical Office of Kosova, Prishtina, January 2006

even in official statistics (and far higher according to unofficial ones).

**Table 5.2.2: Labor Force and Employment by Sex in Kosova**

| Subject | Sex | | Kosova (%) |
|---|---|---|---|
| | Male (%) | Female (%) | |
| Labor force, out of which | 68.1 | 25.3 | 46.2 |
| Employed | 46.8 | 9.9 | 27.9 |
| Unemployed | 21.4 | 15.4 | 18.3 |
| Not belonging to labor force | 58.4 | 84.1 | 71.4 |
| Unemployment rate | 31.5 | 60.7 | 39.7 |

*Source*: Statistical Office of Kosova (2004)

Moreover, in line with our supposition that education is an important factor in Kosova's development and that the spoil effect may make people reluctant towards schooling and working, we see that a high percentage of the population does not belong to the work force and that the unskilled constitute the largest number of registered jobseekers.

**Table 5.2.3: Kosova Jobseekers by Qualification**

| Level of skills | Jobseekers | |
|---|---|---|
| | Number | % |
| Unskilled | 177,943 | 59.0 |
| Semi-unskilled | 12,948 | 4.3 |

54

| | | |
|---|---|---|
| Skilled | 27,557 | 9.1 |
| Secondary school | 78,286 | 26.0 |
| High school | 2,316 | 0.8 |
| University | 2,264 | 0.8 |
| Total | 301,314 | 100.0 |

*Source:* Statistical Office of Kosova (2004)

We have already seen that those with lowest level of education receive the largest amounts of remittances. Obviously the unemployment rates for skilled and relatively well-educated individuals are not as bad as for the unskilled. So the unskilled and the poorly educated are the ones most likely to be affected by the spoil effect, which could be why they would not seek, or at least would be very reluctant to seek, skill upgrading, training, or further education.

---

### Box 4: A Tale of Two Villages[57]

In its research about the impact of remittances on Kosova, the European Stability Initiative (ESI) focuses its case discussion and analysis on two Kosova villages, Cerrce and Lubishte. In land area and in population size, Cerrce and Lubishte are somewhat similar. Cerrce has about 1,980 inhabitants in 300 households and Lubishte has about 2,134 in 229 households. Some 607 of Cerrce's inhabitants and 572 of Lubishte's inhabitants live abroad.

---

[57] *"Cutting the Lifeline: Migration, Families and the Future of Kosova"*, European Stability Initiative, Berlin September 2006 [box contents summarized from this source]

Unlike Lubishte, which lies in South-Eastern Kosova and close to the small town of Viti, Cerrce lies in Western Kosova and is only 2km away from a regional road through which it can connect to Peja, one of the biggest cities in Kosova.

Table 5.2.4: Household Composition for Lubishte and Cerrce

| % | Lubishte | No. of Members | Cerrce | % |
|---|---|---|---|---|
| 10.5 | 24 | 1-4 members | 65 | 21.7 |
| 50.7 | 116 | 5-9 members | 195 | 65.0 |
| 23.6 | 54 | 10-14 members | 28 | 9.3 |
| 14.8 | 34 | 15-30 members | 12 | 4.0 |
| 0.4 | 1 | more than 30 | 0 | 0.0 |
| 100.0 | 229 | Total | 300 | 100.0 |

*Source:* ESI (2006)

When looking at the income for each village, we see a staggering difference. Remittances make up about 55% of total income for Lubishte and only about 21% for Cerrce.

Table 5.2.5: Income for Lubishte and Cerrce

| | Lubishte | | Cerrce | |
|---|---|---|---|---|
| | Income/month (€) | % | Income/month (€) | % |
| Social assistance | 2,394 | 4.3 | 1,798 | 2.4 |
| Kosova pensions | 3,108 | 5.5 | 3,360 | 4.5 |
| Foreign pensions | 2,670 | 4.8 | 4,512 | 6.0 |
| Remittances | 30,576 | 54.8 | 15,833 | 21.1 |
| Economic activities | 17,065 | 30.6 | 49,474 | 66.0 |

| | | | |
|---|---|---|---|
| Total | 55,813 | 100.0 | 74,977 | 100.0 |
| Per capita | 36 | | 57 | |

*Source:* ESI (2006)

In search for more insights into the relation between the spoil effect and labor participation, we refer to the ESI study. As seen from the box above, we notice that Lubishte's migrant population has been very generous and their remittances constitute the most significant source of income for the village, as opposed to Cerrce. Yet, Cerrce's average monthly income per capita is almost twice that of Lubishte. While Cerrce is heavily involved in economic activities (mainly regular employment), Lubishte is not. There could be a number of arguments made as to why Lubishte is much less economically active than Cerrce. But, one of them, and perhaps one of significance, is that the very large amounts of remittances that Lubishte residents receive provides a reason behind their economic passivity — allowing them to leave the labor force.

## 5.3. *An Empirical Quest of the Spoil Effect*

While our previous analyses — both qualitative and even somewhat quantitative — along with a handful of important insights provide a good foundation for our study of the spoil effect, they neither prove nor disprove its existence. Therefore, we turn to household data to study the spoil effect more rigorously and empirically.

Household data in general are known to be hard to work with and sometimes not very compact. Because we focus on Kosova as our case study, we use the World Bank's Living Standard Measurement Survey for Kosova 2000 household datasets. The World Bank's LSMS is very extensive and data is separated into a dozen files. For the purposes of this study, we create our own dataset with data from several of the World Bank LSMS data files. Merging all of these separate files proved to be quite a challenge due to the volume of data and more importantly due to the lack of an individual identification variable (number) for each observation, as some files contained household data and some individual data (see Appendix C for more technical details).

In our dataset, besides a few other secondary variables (such as: who pays for your education, year of birth, etc.), we include the following primary variables for individual respondents (a total of 17,989), which we separate into four categories:

- *Individual/Household Characteristics*: gender, age, household size (in adult equivalents), rural/urban residence;
- *Education Variables*: total years of education, distance to school (km), annual schooling expenditure;
- *Labor Variables*: searching for work in the past seven days, weeks worked in the past twelve months, hours worked in the past year, last payment amount, type of work;
- *Income/Remittance Variables*: total annual remittances, times per year you receive remittances, household members receiving remittances, amount of remittances.

We will embark in our empirical quest of the spoil effect by running a set of simple OLS regressions. As stated earlier, we expect to see a statistically significant negative correlation between remittances and education attainment as well as labor participation. Being acutely aware of key econometric problems that may emerge—such as reverse causality or omitted variables bias—we do not, at this time, make any causal claims. Now we are only seeking to either prove or disprove our initial hypothesis that there exists a negative correlation between remittances and education as well as labor force participation.

The following table presents our regressions' results on the effect of remittances on education attainment.

**Table 5.3.1: Effects of Remittances on Individual Education Attainment**

| School Attainment (years of education) | (1) | (2) | (3) | (4) |
|---|---|---|---|---|
| Household size (in adult equivalents) | -.058 *** (.009) | -.060*** (.009) | -.071*** (.010) | -.060*** (.009) |
| Per equivalent expenditure (month) | .001 (.0003) | .0005 (.0003) | .0001* (.00004) | .0005 (.0003) |
| Amount of total remittances (year) | -.001 *** (.00001) | | | |
| Log (amount of total remittances) | | -.157*** (.024) | -.155*** (.024) | |
| Gender | .029 (.041) | .033 (.041) | .033 (.041) | .033 (.0414076) |
| Age | .763 *** (.005) | .764*** (.005) | .763*** (.005) | .764*** (.005) |
| Type of residence (rural/urban) | .108 ** (.042) | .098** (.042) | .093** (.042) | .099** (.042) |
| Distance to school (km) | .001 (.001) | .002 (.002) | .001 (.001) | .001 (.001) |
| School expenditure (year) | .0002*** (.00005) | .0002*** (.00005) | .0002*** (.00005) | .0002*** (.00005) |
| School expenses | | | .103 (.064) | |

| | (1) | (2) | (3) | (4) |
|---|---|---|---|---|
| paid by someone else | | | | |
| Log (one average remittance amount) | | | | -.167*** (.027) |
| Constant | -3.902 (.137) | -3.884 (.137) | -4.008 (.175) | -3.884 (.137) |
| Observations | 4285 | 4285 | 4285 | 4285 |
| R-squared | 0.8750 | 0.8750 | 0.8751 | 0.8749 |
| Adjusted R-squared | 0.8748 | 0.8747 | 0.8748 | 0.8746 |

Note: * statistically significant at 10%, ** statistically significant at 5%, *** statistically significant at 1%. Standard errors are given in parenthesis.

As seen from Table 5.3.1, regression (1) shows that the amount of total remittances received is negatively correlated with education attainment. This implies (but has not been proven for causal implications yet) that the more remittances one receives, the less likely he is to attain higher levels of education. Moreover, so far we have already seen through our qualitative analysis and data (i.e. interviews, surveys) several reasons about why people never graduate or never go from one level of education to another as long as they receive remittances.

Nevertheless, we acknowledge the fact that our variable of focal interest coefficient (amount of total remittances received) in regression (1) is quite small for inferring practical significance. We are dealing with all absolute data here, which is the reason why the total remittances coefficient in regression (1) above is almost zero — simply because realistically a one DM (Deutsch Mark) increase in remittances cannot have any practical effect on years of schooling. So, now we look at the log of the amount of total remittances received as our variable of concern. And, as regression (2) shows, the coefficient is now strongly statistically significant (at the 99% level). As expected and hypothesized initially, the correlation between remittances and school attainment is negative. Such results are especially reinforced by regression (4) even when we look at the log of one-time average remittance amount received.

Turning to the practical significance of remittances on education attainment and looking at regression (4), we calculate that an increase of one percent in a one-time average remittance transfer is associated with a decrease of 0.45 school days (assuming a year of education is equal to nine calendar months). For instance, the uncle in Germany decides to send his nephew in Kosova €120 instead of €100. It is likely that by sending this extra €20, the good-hearted and generous uncle just made his nephew a bit more reluctant towards attending school — and eventually the nephew misses about nine days of school—hence, the spoil effect. Is it worthwhile to miss nine days of school for €20?

This set of regressions also shows that the household size (in adult equivalents) is statistically significant and negatively correlated with education attainment. The individual's age is positively correlated with education attainment and this could be due to several reasons, one of which is directly related to data. About one-third of the individuals in the data are below the age of 15, which means that they are to be at least finishing elementary school (of eight years) that is mandatory in Kosova. As for school expenditure, while it shows as statistically significant, its practical significance is negligible. Living in an urban area is positively correlated with education attainment and is statistically significant (at the 95% level). Per equivalent expenditure, gender, and distance to school, are shown to be statistically insignificant to education attainment.

On the labor side, the following table presents our regressions' results on the effect of remittances on labor participation for individuals aged between 15 and 64 years.

# Table 5.3.2. Effects of Remittances on Individual Labor Participation

| Labor Participation | Weeks worked in past 12 months (1) | Hours worked per year (2) | Hours worked per year (3) | Hours worked per year (4) |
|---|---|---|---|---|
| Household size (in adult equivalents) | -.041 (.091) | 27.027*** (6.097) | 27.221*** (6.096) | 29.726*** (5.863) |
| Per equivalent expenditure (month) | .013*** (.003) | 2.016*** (.205) | 2.019*** (.206) | 1.978*** (.203) |
| Years of education | .291*** (.069) | 17.19*** (4.603) | 17.202*** (4.603) | 21.667*** (4.364) |
| Log (amount of total remittances) | -.286*** (.077) | -28.206*** (5.087) | | |
| Amount of total remittances | | | | -.0009** (.0003) |
| Gender | 5.873*** (.502) | -178.082*** (33.340) | -176.758*** (33.325) | -176.758*** (33.325) |
| Age | .222*** (.022) | 6.779*** (1.459) | 6.745*** (1.459) | 6.369** (1.292) |
| Type of residence (rural/urban) | 4.841** (.520) | 344.520** (34.321) | 344.668** (34.328) | 348.803** (33.697) |
| Last wage/salary payment | .0003 (.0005) | .176*** (.039) | .176*** (.039) | .179*** (.039) |
| Marital status | -.386** (.124) | -33.532*** (8.152) | -33.377*** (8.151) | -32.226*** (7.803) |
| Log (one average remittance amount) | | | -31.512*** (5.796) | |
| Constant | 15.307 (1.869) | 584.928 (128.122) | 580.558 (128.087) | 439.936 (121.927) |
| Observations | 4396 | 5018 | 5018 | 5018 |
| R-squared | 0.1079 | 0.0865 | 0.0863 | 0.0862 |
| Adjusted R-squared | 0.1060 | 0.0849 | 0.0846 | 0.0846 |

As seen from Table 5.3.2, regression (1) shows a statistically significant and negative correlation of 'weeks worked in the past 12 months,' as our proxy for labor participation, with amount of total remittances received. One other thing to note though is that this variable is mainly focused on work performed in the informal sector—such as housework, self-employment, gardening for profit, handicrafts production, which usually represent traditional areas of work for women in Kosova—hence, the coefficient of gender is positive (being female is positively associated with more work in this category).

The rest of regressions use the hours worked per year as the proxy for labor participation. All of them yield a statistically significant and negative correlation between the dependent variable of our focus and the remittance indicators—total amount of remittances received, and amount of one remittance transfer. As opposed to regression (1), gender plays a different role in regressions (2), (3), and (4): being female is statistically significant and negatively correlated with hours worked per year. This difference emerges because the dependent variable (hours worked per year) now takes into account all formal and informal work performed in a year. The rest of the variables—household size (except in regression (1)), per equivalent expenditure, years of education, age, type of residence, last wage/salary payment (except in regression (1)), and marital status—are all statistically significant across the board.

Two important observations from the coefficients of these variables can be made: living in an urban area is positively correlated with hours of work (which may indicate that there are more work opportunities in urban areas than in rural ones, or that Kosovars have simply abandoned agriculture and farm work); being single is negatively correlated with hours of work per year (which may be due to the fact that a single person carries fewer responsibilities for the welfare of the household as opposed to a married person, who is at least expected to provide for his own dependents).

Turning to the practical significance of the effect of remittances on labor participation, based on the above regressions, we see that, for example, on average an increase of 1% in an average remittance transfer is associated with a decrease of 0.315 hours worked per year. This may not seem very practically significant. But, let's dig a bit deeper. Based on our data, we know that the average hours worked per year is about 1500, and the average times per year a person received remittances is about 3.5. For instance, the sister who lives in the US decides to send her brother in Kosova some $420, instead of the $300 she previously sent (a 40% increase, as now she has a better paying job). She is generous and usually sends her brother money about four times a year. When the brother receives these transfers, he feels more reluctant towards working, and eventually works about 50 hours less per year.

While our simple OLS regressions provide important empirical insights into the spoil effect, as stated earlier, they do not determine the way in which causality goes. Some could argue that one receives more remittances because he is less educated, as opposed to one being less educated because he receives more remittances (which is what we claim to hold). Therefore, in order to address the causality issue more rigorously, we turn to instrumental variables.

Given the limited information about the remittance senders in our dataset, there were not many choices of variables we could use to instrument for remittances. Nevertheless, the dataset provided a variable indicating the country of residence of the migrant sending the remittances. Initially, we decided to use the GDP per capita of the remitter's country of residence as our instrumental variable. It is logical for the GDP per capita of the remitter's country to be positively associated with the amount of remittances he sends home to Kosova. At the same time, the GDP per capita of the remitter's country of residence does not in any way affect the education attainment of the remittance recipient in Kosova. Thus, the GDP per capita of the remitter's country of residence could be a good instrumental variable. However, the dataset identified only a few countries of remitters' residences—Germany, Switzerland, Italy, USA, Albania, Former Yugoslavia, and "Other Western"—leading to a very small degree of variation within this variable, and few observations. As a result, our instrumental variable regressions (Two-Stage Least Squares) did not yield significant results.

Next, we turned to finding another instrumental variable. Another key information that we had in our dataset was the relationship between the remitter and the remittance recipient. So, we established a series of dummy variables indicating this relationship. We then used the relationship between the remitter and the remittance recipient as our instrumental variable for remittances.

The relationship variable is a good instrumental variable because it affects the amount of remittances based on the closeness of relationship between the remitter and the remittance recipient, but it does not directly affect the years of education or labor participation of the remittance recipient, except through remittances.

As shown in the Table 5.3.3, the Two-Stage Least Square regressions using our instrumental variable showed that our relationship dummies make a good instrumental variable and that there is a negative relationship between remittances and both the education attainment and labor participation.

**Table 5.3.3: Instrumental Variables (2SLS) Regressions**

| First Stage Regressions: Amount of Total Remittances (log) | | |
|---|---|---|
| Spouse | 2.218*** | 2.049*** |
| | (.264) | (.378) |
| Child | .881*** | 1.094*** |
| | (.156) | (.241) |
| Parent | 1.902*** | 1.815*** |
| | (.251) | (.329) |
| Grand Parent | 1.161*** | 1.241*** |
| | (.130) | (.196) |
| Brother / Sister | .456*** | .545** |
| | (.128) | (.181) |

|              |            |            |
| ------------ | ---------- | ---------- |
| No Relation  | -.621*     | -.866*     |
|              | (.292)     | (.378)     |
| Constant     | 7.547      | 7.545      |
|              | (.103)     | (.154)     |
| F Prob.      | 30.420     | 16.310     |
| R-squared    | 0.113      | 0.119      |
| N            | 1437       | 731        |

*Instrumental Variables (2SLS) Regression*

|                                                      | Education Attainment (total years of education) | Labor Participation (yearly hours worked) |
| ---------------------------------------------------- | ----------------------------------------------- | ----------------------------------------- |
| Total Remittances (log amount of total remittances)  | -.746*** (.217)                                 | -40.552 (59.383)                          |
| Constant                                             | 14.380 (1.798)                                  | 1766.149 (493.741)                        |

Note: * statistically significant at 10%, ** statistically significant at 5%, *** statistically significant at 1%. Standard errors are given in parenthesis.

**Table 5.3.4: Instrumental Variables (2SLS) Regressions modeled**

**after the OLS Regressions**

|                                                       | Education Attainment [1] (total years of education) | Labor Participation [2] (yearly hours worked) |
| ----------------------------------------------------- | --------------------------------------------------- | --------------------------------------------- |
| Total Remittances (log amount of total remittances)   | -.068 (.532)                                        | -7.911 (64.943)                               |
| Household size (in adult equivalents)                 | .049 (.225)                                         | 12.663 (21.620)                               |
| Per equivalent expenditure (month)                    | .009 (.007)                                         | .604 (.609)                                   |
| Gender                                                | .146 (.690)                                         | -114.112 (101.792)                            |

| | | |
|---|---|---|
| Age | .473***<br>(.068) | |
| Type of residence<br>(rural/urban) | 1.411*<br>(.771) | |
| Distance to school<br>(km) | -.002<br>(.021) | |
| School expenditure<br>(year) | .002*<br>(.001) | |
| Last wage/salary<br>payment | | .519***<br>(.159) |
| Marital status | | -3.319<br>(30.249) |
| Total Years of<br>Education | | 9.839*<br>(4.915) |
| Constant | -3.134<br>(3.020) | 1070.821<br>(506.161) |
| Observations | 53 | 731 |
| R-squared | 0.75 | 0.04 |
| Adjusted R-squared | 0.71 | 0.03 |

(1) IV regression was modeled after the Education OLS Regression (2) in Table 5.3.1.

(2) IV regression was modeled after the Labor OLS Regression (2) in Table 5.3.2.

Note: * statistically significant at 10%, ** statistically significant at 5%, *** statistically significant at 1%. Standard errors are given in parenthesis.

Due to the very few number of observations in the labor regressions in Table 5.3.3, we do not get the desired statistical significance for its coefficient. The same can be noted for the instrumental variable regressions modeled after our OLS regressions for both education and labor participation, as shown in Table 5.3.4. However, if we had a larger number of observations, the coefficients of remittances in the instrumental variable regressions (in Tables 5.3.3 and 5.3.4) would have definitely been statistically significant.

Nevertheless, the bottom line is that the trend of negative correlation between remittances and education as well as labor participation (although not statistically significant in the case of labor participation in Table 5.3.3 and in both cases in Table 5.3.4) is showed even through instrumental variables. Based on the arguments built so far, it can now be stated that remittances are negatively affecting the education attainment of recipients — the more remittances one receives, the less education attainment one will acquire.

Recalling our earlier illustrative examples about the practical significance of the effect of remittances on education and labor participation, we may think that working 50 hours less per year or missing 9 days of school may not be all that problematic if it were to happen only once. But, reluctance towards work and school becomes a habit, as these individuals receive remittances continuously. They start by missing a few days of school and soon enough end up dropping out altogether. They start by missing a few hours of work, and eventually end up not working at all.

Therefore, given that we have empirically proved a negative correlation between remittances and education attainment and labor participation—hence, the spoil effect, we finally turn to a very crucial factor of which the policy makers and even the public need to be acutely aware.

Kosova is now on its way to the "demographic window of opportunity"[58] as its youngest population in Europe enters the labor market. If this spoil effect persists, these young people will neither attain the education nor the experience necessary to be employable in the twenty-first century's globalized economy.

**Figure 5.3.1: The Kosova Student Dilemma**

---

[58] Bloom, D.E., Williamson, J.G. "Demographic Transitions and Economic Miracles in Emerging Asia," *NBER Working Paper No. W6268*, November 1997

As these generations age (being both relatively poorly educated and only semi-skilled or unskilled) and as remittances gradually drop, the burden on Kosova's future generations increases drastically to the point that it may be unbearable.

**Figure 5.3.2: Kosova Population Pyramid**

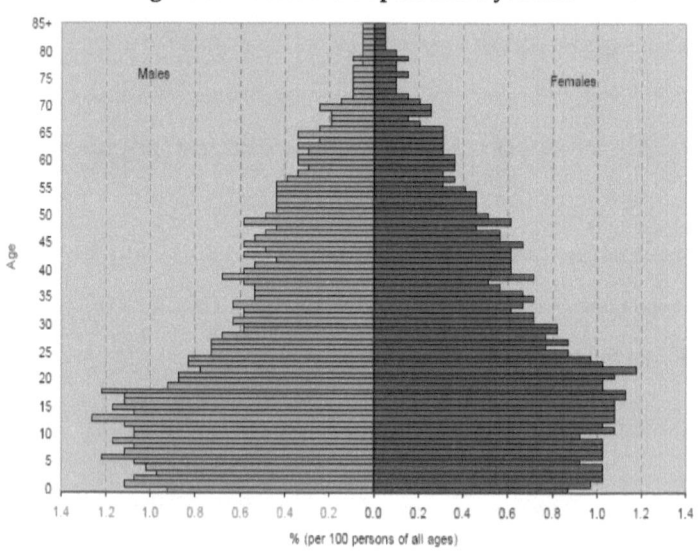

*Source:* Statistical Office of Kosova (2006)

## 6. Conclusions and Policy Recommendations

Our study on Kosova shows that there is a negative correlation between labor participation (proxied by yearly hours of work) and total remittance per individual, and also a negative correlation between

74

education attainment (proxied by total years of education) and total remittance per individual. These results support our theory that the spoil effect creates reluctance towards education and working. This may not be considered particularly good news for the contributors of remittances or the recipients, but it does not say that remittances as such in general are bad. Our findings really call for a more carefully designed way of using remittances.

Nevertheless, one interpretation could be that the Kosova Albanian migrants' very good intentions to support their families and kin to become educated or to not suffer under poverty, and by the same token, to help their country further develop, may also have negative effects, for the long-run at least. These findings should also be given detailed attention by policy makers in Kosova, because it may be the case that the longer the spoil effect persists, the more it hurts the path of human capital build-up in Kosova.

Therefore, the related policy question here is how to make sure that these remittances really serve their good-intentioned aims without bringing about the undesired negative effects. Because of the very nature of the Spoil Effect – as something that is dependent on individual behavior – the ideal solution for this problem requires social reengineering. While social reengineering cannot be easily achieved, we propose the following, more easily implementable, measures that policymakers in Kosova should consider.

*Establishing of a Purpose Specific Payment System (PSPS)*

Considering the fact that Kosova Albanian remitters usually want to support their family's further education, private businesses, and the like, besides simple consumption needs, one way to make sure that the remittances are used for the intended purposes, is to facilitate direct payments to the schools or universities, for instance, if the target of the remittance is education.

Kosova is not a centrally planned economy. It is a market economy. Also, all remittance transfers are private, which leaves very little room for direct government involvement. However, the government can play a role by enacting a policy that requires both public and private institutions of education to facilitate direct payments from abroad for their students who receive remittances. This strategy would result in remittances being used for their intended purposes—minimizing the potential spoil effect.

Similarly, the government should implement the same policy for other institutions such as hospitals.

To help make sure this direct payment system is utilized, the government should also undertake a public information campaign, especially in the major Kosova Albanian diasporas, to make the Kosova migrants aware of the benefits of using the PSPS (the major benefit being the fact that the PSPS mitigates the spoil effect on the part of the recipients).

### Offering Vocational Training

The government should consider vocational schools and training programs as another means by which the large number of Kosovars who are jobless and unskilled, and those dependent on remittances, could be lured into something productive and educational as opposed to staying in cafés.

There are a number of Education Colleges (under the umbrella of the University of Prishtina) located in all seven major cities in Kosova. These colleges, however, only offer traditional teaching degrees, and are public higher education institutions funded by the government. Thus, the government should design and develop vocational training programs focused on technical fields (such as electrics, plumbing, etc), which could be offered by these Education Colleges. The fact that Kosova needs vocational training programs was also underlined as a very important policy priority for the Kosova government at the International Forum on Education held in Prishtina in June 2005 under the auspices of the Prime Minister's Office.[59] Establishing of such programs could lead to a decrease in the number of Kosova's young people using their time unproductively. This policy would also allow the Kosova migrants to make sure that their remittances are put to good use—as they could make the transfers conditional (or directly payable to the school) on the recipient's upgrading of skills (by attending vocational training). The more skilled the recipients become, the better their chances are to find a job in the future.

*Offering Higher Savings Interest Rates*

Considering the fact that the total volume of worker remittances as a share of GDP is considerable, i.e. 15.1% of GDP in 2005,[60] it seems reasonable for the government to establish a Kosovar National Development Bank (KNDB). The mission of the KNDB would be to

[59] Bislimi, Faton, *My Kosovar Journey*, Jalifat Publishing, Houston, Texas, April 2006
[60] *BPK Annual Report 2005*, Banking and Payments Authority of Kosova, Prishtina, June 2006

attract savings—both from Kosovars living in Kosova and receiving money from abroad and from Kosovars abroad, too—which in turn could be used for beneficial and development-oriented projects and other profitable investments. With the support of the government, this bank would offer attractive interest rates for its account holders—this is quite reasonable given the fact that the risk premium is higher in a developing country than a developed one—and it could be likely that the workers abroad would also directly deposit their savings with this bank rather than a western bank.

For individuals in Kosova who receive remittances, the bank savings account would provide a good alternative to spending the received remittances in pure consumption and cafés. If the money is deposited regularly into the savings account, the individual's assets will grow over time—and the individual will not have the luxury to spend as much as he used to before he started depositing his remittances into his savings account. Therefore, the smaller the amount of remittances readily for use by the individual recipient, the smaller the spoil effect.

# Appendix A

Regression results to show a positive correlation between the household expenditure and the total amount of remittances it receives:

Total Household Expenditure (totexp)

| | |
|---|---|
| Household Total Remittances (htotRemit) | 0.146*** |
| | (0.005) |
| Constant | 807.101*** |
| | (3.804) |
| R-squared | 0.049 |
| N | 17979 |

*** statistically significant at the 1% level.

# Appendix B

Tony Bislimi was in Kosova for his KSG internship. In July 2006, he supervised the conduct of simple survey of about 2,500 individuals. The Bislimi Group Education for Peace Scholarships Program assisted with recruiting a group of 12 statistics students of the University of Prishtina to carry out the survey. The funding for the survey and Tony's related work in Kosova was provided by the Albanian American Foundation, New York.

The purpose of the survey was to provide some insights into the income conditions of the people who utilize the many cafés in Kosova. The survey was designed to collect data on the employment status of individuals, their gender, whether they have family members abroad and whether they receive remittances. The survey was carried out in three major Kosova towns: Gjilan (which is known for a large migrant population in Western Europe), Prishtina (capital of Kosova), and Skenderaj (which is known for very small migrant population). Surveyors walked randomly into several cafés in these towns and asked individuals staying therein to respond to the survey. The results of the survey were shown in Table 5.1.3.

# Appendix C

Merging the specific variables we needed to create our Master Spoil Data File was a challenge because the LSMS data files included a household ID but not specific ID for each individual observation. Some LSMS data files had household data and some individual. The problem was the lack of a unique individual ID in the individual level data files.

But, after reading the questionnaire and the data dictionary of the LSMS, we found out that each individual level data file besides the household ID also had an ID code identifying each member of the household. For example, the data file on education had four entries identified with household ID 104 and the ID codes 1, 3, 6 identifying the individual member of the household 104. But, to merge the education data with a similar data file (labor, for instance) we had to have one unique ID for each individual.

We produced this unique individual ID in the following way:
IndivID=HouseholdID*100+HDMemberID

So, for example, the three members of the household 104 on whom we had data on education, now would each have a unique ID: 10401, 10403, 10406. We created this IndivID in all data files containing individual level data and then merged the files following the STATA procedures for merging by unique case ID.

# Appendix D

## *Worker Remittances in Turkey*

Since early 1960s, Turkish workers have migrated to mainly Western Europe and most of them to the Federal Republic of Germany. Since 1960, over 2 million Turks have migrated to work in about 30 countries. After 1970s, Turks started to go to Arabic countries to work, and finally after the independence of Turkish States in Central Asia from the Soviets in late 1980s and early 1990s Turks started to go to ex-soviet republics in search of employment opportunities.

Figure D shows the trend in Turkish workers' remittances for the period of 1984 to 2006. Since 1976, Turkey has had a foreign exchange deposit program offering premium interest rates on foreign currency accounts. Currently, the Central Bank of the Republic of Turkey offers two types of accounts for migrants: foreign currency deposit accounts with credit letter and super foreign exchange accounts. These accounts have been instrumental in attracting workers' remittances to Turkey. To illustrate the reason behind the decline in workers' remittances flowing to Turkey in 2000s, it will be sufficient to have a broad idea about the trend of the interest rates offered on foreign currency accounts: The annual interest rate on EUR/DEM foreign currency deposit accounts with credit letter was 9.5 percent in 1998, later it decreased to 3.75 percent in 2003, and the current interest rate is 2.75 percent. A similar trend exists for the interest rate on the super foreign exchange accounts.

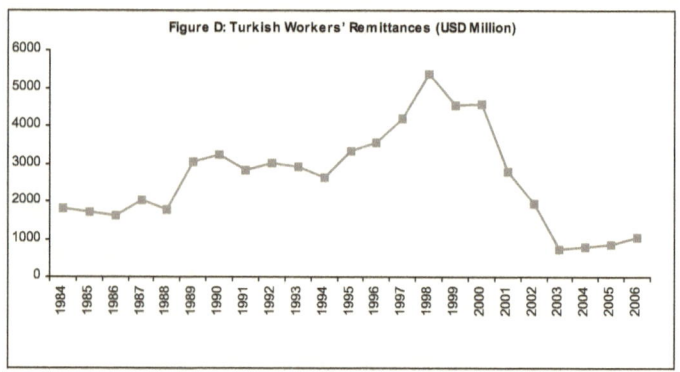

The reason behind the government's effort to attract workers' remittances in 1970s was to finance the import bill of the country, since the export revenues were also too low in 1970s. In line with the increase in the volume of other external financing resources like foreign direct investment and portfolio investments, the relative importance of the workers' remittances in external financing declined. To illustrate this clearly, it is worthwhile to mention that the ratio of workers'

remittances to imports was 19.1 percent in 1976, this declined to 8.6 percent in 2000 and to 0.9 percent in 2006. The reason behind this huge decline is twofold: first is the voluminous increase in Turkish imports; second is the decline in the workers remittances received by the country. To sum up this policy, workers' remittances were influential as an external financing resource especially in 1970s and 1980s. So, the Turkish governments can be given good credit to invent and implement such a policy.

During the 1970s, the Turkish Government tried to channel remittance savings into employment generating activities. The government started programs of Turkish Lira loans for homes, farms and small businesses, with the condition of migrants establishing foreign currency savings accounts with one of the designated Turkish banks. However, as a result of the fact that the private sector offered attractive savings alternatives, such programs of the government to channel remittances into government approved investments could not attract many migrant applicants and so were unsuccessful.

In the beginning of 1970s, labor demand in Western Europe decreased. The Turkish government then signed a bilateral credit program with Federal Republic of Germany triggered by an effort of Germans to promote the departure of Turks back to Turkey. An agreement, signed in 1972, made German funds available to returning Turkish migrants who wished to open a small business in Turkey with the condition that the migrant participated in training programs in both the Federal Republic of Germany and Turkey. But this program could not attract many participants. One analysis showed that such reintegration programs by the host nations to promote returns not attractive enough to encourage migrant participation and were too complicated and too costly for host governments.

*Sources for Appendix D:*

-Central Bank of the Republic of Turkey
-Ministry of Labor and Social Security of the Republic of Turkey
-The policies that Turkey has implemented to use workers' remittances to better effect further development were read and mostly adopted from Neyapti, Bilin, Osman Tuncay Aydas, Kivilcim Metin-Ozcan. "Determinants of Workers Remittances: The Case of Turkey"
http://www.bilkent.edu.tr/~economics/papers/04-05%20DP_Neyapti_Kivilcim_Aydas.pdf
-Martin, P. L. 1992. "The Unfinished Story: Turkish Labor Migration to Western Europe," World Employment Programme Research Working Paper, ILO, Geneva.

## Bibliography:

Adams, Richard and John Page, "Do International Migration and Remittances Reduce Poverty in Developing Countries?" World Development 2005, 33(10): 1645–69

Adams, Richard, "The Economic Uses and Impact of International Remittances in Rural Egypt," *Economic Development and Cultural Change* 39(4): 695–722, 1991

Adams, Richard, "Remittances, Investment, and Rural Asset Accumulation in Pakistan," *Economic Development and Cultural Change* 41(1): 155–73, 1998

Adams, Richard, "Remittances, Household Expenditure and Investment in Guatemala," in *International Migration, Remittances, and the Brain Drain*, ed. Caglar Ozden and Maurice Schiff, World Bank, 2005

Adelman, I., and J. E. Taylor, "Is Structural Adjustment with a Human Face Possible?" *Journal of Development Studies* 26: 387–407, 1992

*Balance of Payments Yearbook*, IMF 2004

Balaj, Barbara, "Kosova's Albanian Diaspora: Blessing or Curse on Economy?" *Beyond Transition*, World Bank 2001 (http://worldbank.org/html/prddr/trans/nd00jan01/pgs15-16.htm, last referenced February 2, 2007)

Bislimi, Faton, *My Kosovar Journey*, Jalifat Publishing, Houston, Texas, April 2006

Bislimi, Faton and Rob Gulick, "Building a Competitive Workforce in Kosova," American Chamber of Commerce in Kosova, Prishtina, June 2005

Bloom, D.E., Williamson, J.G. "Demographic Transitions and Economic Miracles in Emerging Asia," *NBER Working Paper No. W6268*, November 1997

*BPK Annual Report 2005*, Banking and Payment Authority of Kosova, Prishtina, May 2006

*BPK Annual Report 2003*, Banking and Payments Authority of Kosova, Prishtina, March 2004

Bradley, John, and Gerald Knaus, "Towards a Development Plan for Kosovo," ESPIG Policy Paper No. 1, Prishtina, Kosova, August 2004

Central Bank of the Republic of Turkey (www.cbrt.gov.tr)

Cloyes, Shirley DioGuardi, "Jewish Survival in Albania and the Ethics of 'Besa,'" American Jewish Congress, *Congress Monthly*, New York, Jan/Feb 2006

Corker, Robert, Dawn Rehm, Kristina Kostial, "Kosovo: Macroeconomic Issues and Fiscal Sustainability," IMF 2001

Cox Edwards, Alejandro, and Manuelita Ureta, "International Migration, Remittances, and Schooling: Evidence from El Salvador." *Journal of Development Economics* 72(2): 429–61, 2003

"Cutting the Lifeline: Migration, Families and the Future of Kosovo", *European Stability Initiative*, Berlin, September 2006

"Demand Increases for Western Visas," *IliriaPost,* Prishtina, June 29, 2006

Duflo, Esther, "Schooling and Labor Market Consequences of School Construction in Indonesia: Evidence from an Unusual Policy," *American Economic Review* 91(4), September 2001

*Financial and Private Sector Development – Remittances*, World Bank, 2007 (http://web.worldbank.org/WBSITE/EXTERNAL/TOPICS/EXTFI NANCIALSECTOR/EXTPAYMENTREMMITTANCE/0,,contentM DK:21016198~menuPK:2554287~pagePK:210058~piPK:210062~theSi tePK:1943138,00.html, last referenced: February 24, 2007)

"Fischer Scandal: Foreign Minister About to Fall Over Visa Scandal," *KAS Germany* Update No.23, Feb 2005

Funkhouser, Edward, "Migration from Nicaragua: Some Recent Evidence." World Development 20(3): 1209–18, 1992

*Global Economic Prospects*, World Bank, 2006

Hanson, Gordon H., "Emigration, Remittances, and Labor Force Participation in Mexico," IADB, 2006

Itzigsohn, Jose, "Migrant Remittances, Labor Markets, and Household Strategies: A Comparative Analysis of Low-Income Household Strategies in the Caribbean Basin" Social Forces, 74(2):633-655, 1995

"Kasabank – Kosovar Remittances and Migrant Pensions," *Migrant Remittances*, USAID and DFID E-Newsletter, Vol. 2, No. 2, August 2005

*Kosovo Economic Memorandum*, Report No: 28023-KOS, World Bank, Washington, 17 May 2004

*Kosova in Figures 2005*, Statistical Office of Kosova, Prishtina, January 2006

Lucas, Robert, and Oded Stark, "Motivations to Remit: Evidence from Botswana," *Journal of Political Economy* 93: 901–18, 1985

Martin, P. L, "The Unfinished Story: Turkish Labor Migration to Western Europe," *World Employment Programme* Research Working Paper, ILO, Geneva, 1992

Ministry of Labor and Social Security of the Republic of Turkey (www.calisma.gov.tr)

Neyapti, Bilin, Osman Tuncay Aydas, Kivilcim Metin-Ozcan, "Determinants of Workers Remittances: The Case of Turkey," Bilkent University, 2004 (http://www.bilkent.edu.tr/~economics/papers/04-5%20DP_Neyapti_Kivilcim_Aydas.pdf, last referenced: February 18, 2007)

Prishtina International Airport – PRN (official website, www.airportpristina.com, last referenced: December 19, 2006)

*Private Income in Kosova 2003-2005*, Statistical Office of Kosova, Prishtina, September 2006

Ratha, Dilip, "Understanding the Importance of Remittances," World Bank, October 1, 2004 (http://www.migrationinformation.org/Feature/display.cfm?id=2 56, last referenced: February 24, 2007)

Rosenzweig, Mark R., and Oden Stark, "Consumption Smoothing, Migration, and Marriage: Evidence from Rural India," *Journal of Political Economy* 97(4): 906–26, 1989

Statistical Office of Kosova, Prishtina, 2005

UMMIK Home Page - http://www.unmikonline.org/intro.htm (last referenced February 4, 2007)

Woodruff, Christopher, and Rene Zenteno, "Remittances and Microenterprises in Mexico," *Graduate School of International Relations and Pacific Studies*, University of California–San Diego, 2001 http://sccie.ucsc.edu/documents/working_papers/2001/Remittan ces_Mexico.pdf, last referenced: February 2, 2007)

Yang, Dean, "International Migration, Human Capital, and Entrepreneurship: Evidence from Philippine Migrant's Exchange Rate Shocks," *Research Program on International Migration and Development,* DECRG, Policy Research Working Paper 3578, World Bank, 2004

# DECENTRALIZATION IN KOSOVA:

## A Crosscutting Perspective

**Note:**
Specific knowledge of and references to particular pieces of Kosova legislation (such as UNMIK Regulations, Kosova Laws, etc.) come from my work as a consultant with USAID / RTI International during the summer of 2006 in Prishtina, Kosova.

# DECENTRALIZATION IN KOSOVA:

## *A Crosscutting Perspective*

### 1. Introduction

Government, be it local, national, or federal, is viewed in different ways by different people. It is very hard to find a particular and universally accepted definition of government. Some governments are considered good and some not so good. One of the founding fathers of America, Thomas Paine, whose ideas were used by Jefferson in drafting the Declaration of Independence of the United States of America, a document that even today stands out as an example of establishing a good government based on the free will of the people – a government for the people, by the people, and from the people, said:

> *Some writers have so confounded society with*
>
> *government, as to leave little or no distinction between*
>
> *them; whereas they are not only different, but have*

*different origins. Society is produced by our wants, and government by our wickedness; the former promotes our happiness positively by uniting our affections, the latter negatively by restraining our vices. The one encourages intercourse, the other creates distinctions. The first is a patron, the last a punisher.*[61]

While said a very long time ago, Paine's remarks are of importance even today. Societies strive for good governments. Good governments of any level in turn provide no harm for their respective societies. Undoubtedly, all levels of government should be in service to their citizens. The first level of government, however, should be the most efficient and welcoming.

Local government is usually the first level of government that citizens interact with. It is a form of government with limited powers and authority. Most of the time, local governments are under some kind of supervision from a national or state government. As in any other modern state, institutions of local government have been designed and are functioning in Kosova, too.

---

[61] Paine, Thomas, *Of the Origin and Design of Government in General. With Concise Remarks on the English Constitution*, Philadelphia: February 14, 1776

This paper, however, looks at the plan for decentralization in Kosova from a crosscutting perspective—from sound legislation and economic development points of view—outlaying some basic understanding of institutions and legislation (and its problems) in Kosova with special focus put on local government.

## 1.1. A Historical Note on Kosova

Kosova, an equally constituent part of the Yugoslavian Federation, was illegally and unwillingly stripped of its autonomous and constituent status within the Federation in 1989 by Belgrade, and as a result became one of the poorest and least developed parts of Yugoslavia, and even Europe. The decade of the 1990s marked a remarkable civil resistance of ethnic Albanians, who constitute over 90 % of Kosova's two million people, against the Serbian apartheid.

But, this civil resistance and the belief that the civilized world would come to support Kosova Albanians in their quest for freedom started to fade in the late 1990s. By 1997 armed guerilla Albanian groups emerged. The support for the armed resistance took a steep increase in 1998 when the Kosova Liberation Army (KLA) became publicly and officially the armed movement of Kosova Albanians fighting for freedom. The emergence of KLA triggered the Serb forces to undertake massive military offensives throughout Kosova during late 1998 and early 1999, resulting in mass murders and brutal expulsions. Such a grand-scale ethnic cleansing in the heart of Europe could no longer be  tolerated, bringing about NATO's intervention.

Until NATO's first war in the history of its existence, very few people knew where Kosova was or anything else about it. However, scenes of brutality and genocide committed by Serbian forces against the ethnic Albanian civilian population of Kosova shook the world in early 1999 and made Kosova a violently radiant place on the world map. To stop this unfolding "New Holocaust" — as many personalities familiar with the history of the Balkans and that of Kosova have put it — NATO engaged in a 79-day air strike campaign against Serbian forces.

Since NATO's successful military intervention, which resulted in all Serbian forces being withdrawn from Kosova, the country was put under the United Nations administration.  According to the UNSC Resolution 1244 of 10 June 1999, the UN Mission in Kosova (UNMIK) was called upon to:[62]

- perform basic civilian administrative functions;

- promote the establishment of substantial autonomy and self-government in Kosova;

- facilitate a political process to determine Kosova's future status;

- coordinate humanitarian and disaster relief of all international agencies;

- support the reconstruction of key infrastructure;

- maintain civil law and order;

- promote human rights; and

- assure the safe and unimpeded return of all refugees and displaced persons to their homes in Kosova.

However, UNMIK was neither mandated, nor sufficiently capable to assist Kosova in its much needed

---

[62] United Nations Mission in Kosovo (official web-page: unmikonline.org)

development effort. That is a task that was left to the European Union.

But, Kosova's economy was not only underdeveloped to begin with; it had also been harshly damaged for over a decade during the Serbian rule. As also noted by IMF, "the war provided a further setback to output and the quality and capacity of the infrastructure. Damage to the housing stock was particularly extensive, but the main utilities (power, telecommunications) also suffered considerable damage, as did some of the already dubiously viable industrial concerns."[63]

During the Serbian rule of the 1990s, Kosova Albanians were massively dismissed from public jobs. Being a socialist economy, most of the jobs in Kosova were in the public domain. So, this massive dismissal of Kosova Albanians created huge unemployment, which naturally fed into an increase in poverty. Being an Albanian in Kosova during the period of Serbian domination was an excuse not only to be dismissed from a job, but also to be

---

[63] Robert Corker, Dawn Rehm, Kristina Kostial, "Kosovo: Macroeconomic Issues and Fiscal Sustainability," IMF 2001

denied any public services—some as essential as health care and education.

Nevertheless, Kosova Albanians managed to establish a parallel state[64] run by a government-in-exile, which was successful in collecting voluntary, yet very significant amounts of money, into the Republic of Kosova Fund—named the "3 percent." This "3-percent" fund was mainly used to fund an underground education system and a quasi-public healthcare system. It also provided for a social welfare system to help those in extreme poverty.

Being a society with close family ties and very non-individualistic, Kosova Albanians in the diaspora played the most crucial role in ensuring the economic survival of the Albanians inside Kosova. Initially, only the diaspora members contributed into the "3-percent" fund. In addition, migrant Kosova Albanians, mainly residing in Western Europe, provided substantial financial assistance to their family, relatives, and friends in Kosova, especially over the decade of the 1990s.

---

[64] Howard Clark, *Civil Resistance in Kosovo*, Pluto Press: 2000

## 2. Kosova Institutions and Decentralization

After the establishment of UNMIK in Kosova (a UN protectorate since June 1999), institutions of self-government were created. In 2000 and 2002, Kosova successfully held free and democratic local elections (municipalities represent the local level of government), and in 2001 and 2004, it successfully also held national elections. Today, Kosova has a National Assembly (legislature), Government (executive), President, an independent Judiciary consisting of local, district, and supreme courts, and a Central Banking Authority.

However, due to the conflict of the past, Kosova remains a fragile society ethnically. The Serbian minority still hopes for the return of the Serbian rule over Kosova, and continuously boycotts newly established, democratic Kosova institutions.

The international community (mainly UNMIK and EU) has repeatedly insisted on decentralization as a means by which the Serbian minority's integration into the new society in Kosova can be achieved. It is believed that giving more power over local affairs to Serbian municipalities in Kosova may ensure a progressive integration of this minority in all aspects of life in Kosova. A decentralization plan has now become an integral and major part of the Comprehensive Proposal for Kosova Final Status Settlement by the UN Special Envoy for Kosova Final Status, Mr. Martti Ahtisaari, a former Finnish president.[65] The Ahtisaari proposal provides for a "supervised independence" for Kosova as a way to meet the Kosova Albanian majority rightful demands, and a detailed decentralization plan to meet the Serbian minority demands. This proposal, backed by the US and EU, is now being debated at the UN Security Council and its approval — given Russia's non-use of veto — is expected to happen in June. The Kosova National Assembly has already approved the Ahtisaari proposal in April, and thereby has committed to the implementation of its decentralization plan, among others.

In this context, and given the complexity of Kosova's past and present, establishing a solid local government has been a challenge for both the locals and internationals working in Kosova. This challenge has not yet been overcome completely. On top of the required

---

[65] Martti Ahtisaari, "Comprehensive Proposal for Kosovo Final Status Settlement," UNOSEK, Vienna, March 2007

decentralization, a major part of this remaining challenge is the legislation on local government in Kosova.

The new institutions of local self-government in Kosova, after their creation in 2000 by UNMIK and through Kosova's first democratic, free and internationally recognized and praised local elections of October 2000, have seen major changes in their functioning and further consolidation.

At the time that Kosova central level government institutions were created – i.e. Ministries – the powers of municipalities have been significantly interfered with and in many cases even overtaken or severely curtailed by such Central Authority agencies.

In order for Kosova to have a modern local government, it has to have a modern legislation based on European standards (such as the European Charter of Local Self Government adopted by the Council of Europe). This Charter should to be truly observed in drafting Kosova's new local government legislation, especially in light of the upcoming decentralization plan, because as we will see later in this paper, many powers that are vested in municipalities by the base legislation on Kosova's local government – UNMIK Regulation 2000/45 on the Self-Government of Municipalities in Kosova, which refers to the Charter as the basis for giving municipalities powers – have been curtailed by central authority agencies.

Therefore, no decentralization of any kind will be a success if Kosova does not first establish a sound legal foundation in general and one for its local government in particular during which process special attention must be paid to the economic development component of municipalities and Kosova as whole.

## 2.1. Laws in Kosova and the Lack of a Sound Legal Foundation

Given the yet undefined status of Kosova as a legal entity in the international community, the legislation that Kosova applies today is of five different categories:

- International covenant and documents as enumerated in the Constitutional Framework of Kosova;[66]

- Yugoslavian and Kosova provincial laws of pre-1989;

- Non-discriminatory Yugoslavian and Kosova provincial laws of post-1989;

---

[66] UNMIK Regulation 2001/9 on a Constitutional Framework for Provisional Self-Government in Kosovo (Preamble), 15 May 2001.

- UNMIK Regulations along with Administrative Directions and Instructions;
- Laws adopted by the Assembly of Kosova.

This very fact provides ground for misinterpretation of legislation and conflicting as well as contradictory provisions. While such a multi-layered legislation remains applicable in Kosova, its effects – mainly negative – are inevitable to the whole of Kosova's government in general, and especially to its local government. Furthermore, UNMIK Regulation 1999/24, article 3, provides that particular provisions of post-1989 Yugoslavian laws are to be applicable in Kosova[67] – however, the provision does not define what these particular former Yugoslavian legal provisions are or what the determining factor is for a legal provision or a law to be considered non-discriminatory. Also, not all of the pre-1989 Yugoslavian laws are non-discriminatory when it comes to their being applied in today's Kosova.

Therefore, there is a clear need for quick completion of new legislation that suits Kosova's current and future needs as a new entity.

But, new legislation being produced for Kosova is heavily affected if not completely produced by foreigners.

---

[67] UNMIK Regulation 1999/24 on the Law Applicable in Kosovo, Section 3.

One could notice different legal orders being applied in different towns in Kosova depending on the NATO forces deployed there. For example, if you go to Prizren (west of Kosova), a German area of responsibility, you notice a sense of German culture and legal traditions being "transplanted" into Prizren's institutions of local government. If you go to Gjilan (south-east of Kosova), however, where Americans are in charge, you cannot but notice the American-based rule of law in the Gjilan institutions.

To make things even more complex, these legal transplants are not only happening at the local level, but also at the national one. Teams of lawyers from the US and many EU countries work in Kosova through different international NGOs and inter-governmental organizations to help Kosova build a western-like legal system. Some argue that this kind of transplantation of legal order into Kosova from the West helps Kosova come closer to Western and EU standards. While it has been shown that "countries that have developed legal orders internally, adapted the transplanted law, and/or had a population that was already familiar with basic principles of the transplanted law have more effective legality than countries that received foreign law without any similar predispositions,"[68] it still remains to be seen if Kosova really fits the category of countries where a transplanted legal order will have more effective legality.

As for the impact on economic development, the same study on the effects of legal transplants by Berkowitz et al., shows that "the transplanting process has a strong indirect effect on economic development via its impact on legality, while the impact of particular legal families is weaker and not robust to alternative legality measures." In the case of Kosova, this means that it really does not matter whether the legal transplants are coming from a common law (UK for instance) or a civil law based system (France for instance) as far as economic development is concerned. But, what matters here is legality. The fact that Kosovars in general have welcome the NATO peacekeeping mission and most of the values that came with it provides some grounds for hope that these transplants will have more legality. Consequently, one can expect that because these transplants have more legality, they will have a more positive effect on the development of Kosova. But, the critical question here remains whether Kosova will be able to properly adopt these transplants in

---

[68] Daniel Berkowitz, Katharina Pistor, and Jean-Francois Richard, "Economic Development, Legality, and the Transplant Effect," *European Economic Review*, vol. 47 (2003)

a uniform way that suits its future as a multiethnic society – that is to say, whether Kosova will be able to benefit from these transplants and truly come closer to EU and Western standards, especially in light of the decentralization plan that Kosova has to implement as part of the Comprehensive Proposal for Kosova Final Status Settlement.

Because of this complex decentralization process that runs mainly across ethnic lines, it may be that all the legal transplants that have happened so far at the local level will be hard to standardize nationally—because it may the case that some legal order in the field of property rights has been established in Prizren based on the German system, and the national legal order in that same field has been established based on the US system, and reconciling the two will not be an easy task. As a result, Kosova will face a legal fragmentation that may then become a barrier to a successful decentralization—because of the inability of a national government to apply a uniform law across the country from where local institutions, as independent as they may be, would derive their powers and authority—and also have a negative impact on the overall development of the country.

Therefore, establishing a new legal order through these various transplants and the multi-layered applicable legislation present crucial challenges for Kosova, which are to be overcome before a successful decentralization can be carried out.

## 2.2. Decentralization and Local Government Legislation

Besides creating a sound legal foundation for its institutions in general, Kosova must in particular have functional local government legislation before it can embark on the decentralization plan as required in the Ahtisaari proposal. Decentralization is deemed a means by which local authorities, and thereby local communities, are given a great degree of power and decision-making over their own local affairs, always within the limits of a national applicable law. If decentralization is done along ethnic lines in a country with a history of ethnic conflict, then it only provides for further division and malfunction of government for the country as whole, which would beat the very key goal of the Ahtisaari proposal — to build a multiethnic Kosova.[69] Furthermore, such decentralization would also have negative effects on the overall economic development of the country.[70]

Looking deeper into the system of local government in Kosova, one notices the tendency to have a European system of local government, which in and of itself should provide for enough local powers and authority without needing a special decentralization process. It can thus be said that Kosova has made enormous efforts to establish democratic, effective, and independent institutions of local self-government according to European standards. In this context, the base regulation mandating local government in Kosova, UNMIK Regulation 2000/45 provides that the institutions of local self-government in Kosova are established based on the European Charter of Local Self Government.[71]

Given that local government in Kosova has been established in accordance with the European Charter of Local Self Government (hereafter referred as the "Charter"), then it is important that several key provisions

---

[69] Martti Ahtisaari, "Comprehensive Proposal for Kosovo Final Status Settlement," UNOSEK, Vienna, March 2007

[70] "A Toolbox to Respond to Conflict and Build Peace," *Creative Associates International*, Washington, DC, 2007

[71] UNMIK Regulation 2000/45 on Self Government of Municipalities in Kosovo (Preamble), 11 August 2000: The UNMIK Official Gazette

of the Charter are fully observed. One of the principles of the Charter is the principle of subsidiary.[72] In plain language, this means that local government is to be established not only as an auxiliary, contributory, supplementary means of government, which carries out tasks that can be completed within the local government territory, but also and more importantly, this Charter is based on the premise that the institutions of local government are established as autonomous and self-governing units deriving their powers from the citizens, and not only directly from the central government or its agencies.[73] This principle then provides for public tasks to be carried out by municipalities as the most local level of government and closest to citizens.

Moreover, another important principle of good local self-government, as established in the Charter, is the principle of financial independence, as a right that municipalities are to have in order to regulate their own local affairs within the territory over which they have jurisdiction.[74] Local affairs are considered matters over which municipalities (as a form of local government) do

---

[72] European Charter on Local Self Government, Article 4, Par 3

[73] Robert Muharremi, "The Process of Decentralization in Kosovo," *USAID Local Government Initiative*, Prishtina, Kosovo, 2005

[74] European Charter on Local Self Government, Article 9

have full authority and discretion.[75] Local affairs are thus managed by the local government, which decides whether or not a public task is considered a local affair and if so when, how, and if the local government will fulfill it.

However, the management of such local affairs by the local government does not grant local authorities absolute control over these affairs, but rather gives them a level of decision-making right within the limits of the applicable law. While local authorities are independent in a form when it comes to managing their own local affairs, the national laws of Kosova should serve as safeguards for proper and legal exercise of authority by all levels of government, including the institutions of local self-government in Kosova, a best practice that is also established in the Charter.[76]

To ensure that local self-government is effective and can exercise its rights to the fullest extent of the law, local government has to have the ability of recourse to judicial remedies as a necessary means to protect unlawful interferences by any central level authority with the local authorities' rights to self-government.[77]

---

[75] European Charter on Local Self Government, Article 4, Par 2

[76] European Charter on Local Self Government, Article 3, Par 1

[77] European Charter on Local Self Government, Article 11

Now, these principles as outlined in the Charter are also envisioned in the Ahtisaari proposal decentralization plan, except that decentralization would be done almost entirely along ethnic lines. But, one key concern here is that there must be legal and enforceable guarantees across the entire country as far as economic property is concerned. While we would like to keep the local government as independent as possible from the central authorities, we must also insist in the central government's assurance for credible protection of economic property. Such an approach would be in line with the notion of "market preserving federalism," which has been known to be important for growth - as in China, for instance.[78] For local governments to be able to exercise their autonomous powers, they also have to have a sufficient level of economic development. Crucial to economic development is protection of property rights. Hence, it is important that uniform national laws are applicable as far as economic property is concerned. If local governments fail in the field of economic development, then they have also failed in their effective governance as well. Being financially sustainable is key to

---

[78] B.R. Weingast, "The Economic Role of Political Institutions – Market-preserving Federalism and Economic Development," *Journal of Law, Economics & Organization*, vol. 11, 1995

any independent local government. The decentralization plan for Kosova in its current form does not provide good grounds for financial sustainability of the new Serb-majority municipalities it creates. While these new municipalities feed the political appetites of local Serbs for more local control, they do not help the overall development of Kosova or even these localities themselves. Therefore, it is in the best interest of both Kosova as whole and the new Serb-majority municipalities to be created only based on sound economic prospects and under the general supervision and guarantees of central authorities at least in the field of economic property protection according to a market-preserving decentralization plan in this case.

## 2.3. Current Problems – Local Government Legislation and Economic Development

To further clarify and illustrate the lack of a sound legislation foundation for local government in Kosova, and to see how this affects economic development, we turn to practical and present problems.

It is usual that when a new legal entity is being established, such as in the case of Kosova, there will inevitably be problems with legislation – such as legal contradictions, conflicting provisions, and gaps. Focusing on the local government legislation of Kosova, some of the core problems consist of:

(i)     *political issues*, which rise from a tendency of central authorities to take away from municipalities powers vested in them by UNMIK Regulation 2000/45 on the Self-Government of Municipalities in Kosova;

(ii)    and *technical issues*.

For a better understanding of political issues and their effects on issues of local government in Kosova, we turn to a brief analysis of some of the critical powers of municipalities, such as property rights, etc.

Even though municipalities are entitled to manage their own local affairs, even in the field of property that belongs to a given municipality,[79] the establishment of the Kosova Trust Agency (KTA) through UNMIK Regulation 2002/12 has negatively and significantly impacted the

---

[79] UNMIK Regulation 2000/45, Section 3.1 (h)

ability of municipalities to manage property affairs within their territory.

The issue of property rights and management is a crucial issue for which the current legislation leaves the municipality with no say. Besides the KTA, the establishment of the Kosova Cadastral Agency[80] too has also left the municipality without the ability to manage the property that is individually and privately owned within its territory. A municipality without any authority on property rights is in no position to govern effectively.

Therefore, between Regulation 2000/45, Regulation 2002/12 (on the establishment of the Kosova Trust Agency), and Regulation 2004/4 (on the promulgation of the Law on Cadastre adopted by the Assembly of Kosova), the competences for property management and property rights have been interlinked and contradicted, leaving the municipality bare of any property control and management mechanisms or competences.

According to Regulation 2000/45, the municipality is empowered with property management and property

---

[80] UNMIK Regulation 2004/4 on the promulgation of the Law on Cadastre adopted by the Assembly of Kosovo

rights of the municipal property within its territory.[81] But, with the creation of the Kosova Trust Agency, the municipality can manage no public property or municipal property without official permission by KTA. Therefore, this kind of a three-level (KTA, Cadastral Agency of Kosova, Municipality) property management and property rights for public or municipality owned property causes dysfunction and ineffectiveness in local government's objectives to better meet its citizens' needs and demands.

This lack of power and authority over municipal property is absolutely a barrier for local economic development. Consequently, an undeveloped municipality will be a financially unsustainable municipality, thus affecting negatively the overall development of the country as whole.

A very similar practice of such three-layered property management is applied when it comes to municipal-owned property dedicated for social sheltering. According to Regulation 2000/45, article 3(h), social services and sheltering is a responsibility of the local

---

[81] UNMIK Regulation 2000/45 on the Local Self-Government of Municipalities in Kosovo, Section 3, Par. 1, (h). 11 August 2000: The UNMIK Official Gazette

government.[82] For instance, in 2005 the Municipality of Suhareke came to an agreement with KTA to turn a municipal-owned building into a shelter for the poor. But, the UN Habitat – the Directorate on Housing and Property Issues[83] – intervened and halted the process, which clearly represents another arbitrary intervention in violation of both Regulation 2000/45 and KTA decision to allow the municipality to manage this specific piece of municipal-owned property.[84] UNMIK Regulation 2000/60 on the Housing and Property Directorate does also fall in contradiction with UNMIK Regulation 2004/4 (Law on Cadastre), since while the latter states that all issues related to property transactions should be resolved by the competent courts in the jurisdictions where these issues are raised, the former gives the Housing and Property Directorate of Kosova (Habitat) full decision-making authority that prevails over that of a court in property issues. Both regulations, however, interfere with municipality's right to manage its property.

Similar instances where municipalities are banned from or interfered with exercising powers granted to them

[82] UNMIK Regulation 2000/45 on the Local Self-Government of Municipalities in Kosovo, Section 3, Par. 1, (k). 11 August 2000: The UNMIK Official Gazette

[83] UNMIK Regulation 2000/60 on the Housing and Property Directorate of Kosovo

[84] Suhareke Briefing Note – from my personal meeting with municipal officials in Suhareke

by UNMIK Regulation 2000/45 are countless – even in the field of management of public services and utilities (controlled by KTA), socially and publicly owned enterprises (SOEs and POEs now being privatized by KTA), etc. As for the already privatized SOEs and POEs that belonged to municipalities, particular legal provisions are to be adopted giving municipalities a way to collect some tax revenue from them. This is not to say that additional taxes are to be put in place for these SOEs and POEs, but rather that a share of the taxes that they pay to the Consolidated Budget of Kosova be given directly to the municipal budget.

And, while the privatization process should continue, it must take into account the considerations of municipalities, if they are expressing the best interests of their citizens, when it comes to future rounds of privatization of municipality owned enterprises and other SOEs and POEs with special impact in the lives of a municipality's residents.

Evidently, the establishment of KTA has then not only affected the property rights of municipalities, but as aforementioned it has also deprived the municipalities of their control over enterprises that are charged with providing public utilities. According to UNMIK

Regulation 2002/12 on the establishment of KTA, all publicly or socially owned enterprises (POEs and SOEs) are put under direct control of the Kosova Trust Agency.[85] Given that municipal enterprises that are charged with providing public services and utilities are publicly owned, it is evident then that they fall automatically under the control of KTA. In this case, the municipality is deprived of an essential responsibility (granted through UNMIK Regulation 2000/45), which not only affects the living standard of its citizens, but also the effectiveness of local government as well as its sources of internal (municipal) revenue collection. If the municipalities were in control of their public services and utilities enterprises, their municipal budgets could have been larger and thus more or better services could have been provided to their citizens.

In view of the interferences that the establishment of KTA has brought about for municipalities, it can be said that local economic development is almost impossible under the current legislation – due to the fact that KTA manages all property, SOEs, and POEs in all of Kosova's municipalities. Given that one of the major issues for the

---

[85] UNMIK Regulation 2002/12 on the establishment of the Kosovo Trust Agency, Section 5.1.

institutions of local self-government in Kosova is the high rate of unemployment, creating new jobs requires a sustainable local economic development plan, which can only be achieved when municipalities as the most local institutions of self-government in Kosova become in charge of truly managing their local affairs, especially those related to property management.

As for technical issues with local government legislation in Kosova, the following is a list of major problems:

- multi-layered applicable legislation
- lack of well researched law drafting practices
- lack of a regulatory impact assessment mechanism
- lack of sufficient professional lawyers in central authority bodies
- lack of legislation compatibility assurance mechanism
- translation problems (when laws are transplanted through "copy & paste")
- unclear provisions, contradictions and legal gaps

One key to the decentralization plan in the Ahtisaari proposal is inter-municipal arrangements—especially the right it grants the Serb-majority municipalities to cooperate with their counterparts in Serbia proper and even the Serbian state. In this context, the current base legislation regulating local government in Kosova completely lacks appropriate provisions on such arrangements. The association of municipalities to foster cooperation and better serve their citizens is a right granted to municipalities by the European Charter of Local Self-Government, which UNMIK Regulation 2000/45 on Self-Government of Municipalities in Kosova refers to.

Section 10 of the Charter stipulates that:[86]

*1. Local authorities shall be entitled, in exercising their powers, to co-operate and, within the framework of the law, to form consortia with other local authorities in order to carry out tasks of common interest.*

*2. The entitlement of local authorities to belong to an association for the protection and promotion of their common interests and to belong to an international*

---

[86] European Charter on Local Self Government, Article 10

*association of local authorities shall be recognized in each State.*

*3. Local authorities shall be entitled, under such conditions as may be provided for by the law, to co-operate with their counterparts in other States.*

While Kosova should recognize the right of its municipalities to associate among themselves or with their counterparts in other states, it should also provide specific provisions as to the inter-municipal arrangements, so that it creates a "framework of the law." Therefore, it is imperative for Kosova to immediately adopt such a framework of the law regarding the right of municipalities to associate, so no one municipality or a group of municipalities can misuse the Charter-granted right for interests other than those stipulated in the Charter. This "framework of the law" should also specifically stipulate that any association or cooperation of Kosova municipalities with counterparts outside of Kosova's own borders (i.e. international) will be under legal supervisory powers of the central authority, or more specifically the Ministry of Local Government Administration (MLGA).

## 3. What Next?

In light of all these legislation problems present in the current Kosova local government legislation and their negative impact on economic development, especially at the local level, it becomes clear that any decentralization plan (much less one along ethnic lines in a post-ethnic conflict country) will not be successful. This is why Kosova first needs to establish a sound legislation foundation (standardizing legal transplants at the national level where necessary) and then engage in a decentralization plan with particular attention being paid to fostering economic development.

The following recommendations may, therefore, help in this process:

- Establish a Legislation Compatibility Office (LCO), which would ensure the compatibility of all pieces of legislation made applicable in Kosova. This office should be staffed by professional legal experts and lawyers specialized in law drafting and research;
- Establish an Accuracy Unit within the LCO that ensures translation accuracy of laws in all

official languages in Kosova (Albanian, Serbian, and English).

- Train ministry legal officers and municipal legal advisers in legal drafting and research;

- Select international legal experts with particular experiences in the region's legal traditions, preferably with legal experience in Kosova particularly, to serve as directors and managers of the LCO and its Units and along with their local counterparts to help ensure sound and effective "legal transplants" where necessary;

- Establish a Legislation Standards Unit within the LCO, which would ensure that all existing and new legislation pertaining to the local government in Kosova is in full compliance and accordance to international norms and standards and other charters and documents from adherence to which Kosova benefits.

- The powers vested in KTA should be relaxed so that municipalities become at least a partner in deciding for the fate of municipal properties as well as SOEs and POEs of special interest to their citizens. Municipalities should be given more powers and responsibilities in the field of property rights and management, as this is an area of municipal responsibility provided by Regulation 2000/45. KTA's powers presently curtail local government's powers significantly.

- As for the already privatized SOEs and POEs that belonged to municipalities, particular legal provisions are to be adopted giving municipalities a way to collect some tax revenue from them.

Kosova will become a fully functional democracy, a successfully decentralized government, and a multiethnic society when its legal and political institutions are built upon the fundamental premises of an effective legal order suitable for the country's particular needs and traditions, and a sustainable economic development prospect.

# Bibliography

_____,"A Toolbox to Respond to Conflict and Build Peace," *Creative Associates International*, Washington, DC, 2007 (last referenced May 4, 2007: http://www.caii-dc.com/CAIIStaff/Dashboard_GIROAdminCAIIStaff/Dashboard_CAIIAdminDatabase/resources/ghai/toolbox20.htm)

Ahtisaari, Martti, "Comprehensive Proposal for Kosovo Final Status Settlement," UNOSEK, Vienna, March 2007

Berkowitz, Daniel and Katharina Pistor, Jean-Francois Richard, "Economic Development, Legality, and the Transplant Effect," *European Economic Review*, vol. 47, 2003

Clark, Howard, *Civil Resistance in Kosovo*, Pluto Press: 2000

Croker, Robert, Dawn Rehm, Kristina Kostial, "Kosovo: Macroeconomic Issues and Fiscal Sustainability," IMF 2001

European Charter on Local Self Government, *Council of Europe*, Strasbourg, October 15, 1985

Muharremi, Robert, "The Process of Decentralization in Kosovo," *USAID Local Government Initiative*, Prishtina, Kosovo, 2005

Paine, Thomas, *Of the Origin and Design of Government in General. With Concise Remarks on the English Constitution*, Philadelphia: February 14, 1776

UNMIK Regulation 1999/24 on the Law Applicable in Kosovo, 12 December1999

UNMIK Regulation 2000/45 on Self Government of Municipalities in Kosovo (Preamble), 11 August 2000

UNMIK Regulation 2000/60 on the Housing and Property Directorate of Kosovo, 31 October 2000

UNMIK Regulation 2001/9 on a Constitutional Framework for Provisional Self-Government in Kosovo (Preamble), 15 May 2001

UNMIK Regulation 2002/12 on the establishment of the Kosovo Trust Agency, 13 June 2002

UNMIK Regulation 2004/4 on the promulgation of the Law on Cadastre adopted by the Assembly of Kosovo, 18 February 2004

Weingast, B.R. "The Economic Role of Political Institutions – Market-preserving Federalism and Economic Development," *Journal of Law, Economics & Organization*, vol. 11, 1995

# KOSOVA:

## The Making of a European State
## or Just a State in Europe?

# KOSOVA

## *The Making of a European State or Just a State in Europe?*

### 1. Introduction

Government, be it local, national, or federal, is viewed in different ways by different people. It is very hard to find a particular and universally accepted definition of government. Some governments are considered good and some not so good. One of the founding fathers of America, Thomas Paine, whose ideas were used by Jefferson in drafting the Declaration of Independence of the United States of America, a document that even today stands out as an example of establishing a good government based on the free will of the people – a government for the people, by the people, and from the people, said:

> *Some writers have so confounded society with*
>
> *government, as to leave little or no distinction*

*between them; whereas they are not only*

*different, but have different origins. Society is*

*produced by our wants, and government by our*

*wickedness; the former promotes our happiness*

*positively by uniting our affections, the latter*

*negatively by restraining our vices. The one*

*encourages intercourse, the other creates*

*distinctions. The first is a patron, the last a*

*punisher.*[87]

While said a very long time ago, Paine's remarks are of importance even today. Societies strive for good governments. Good governments of any level in turn provide no harm for their respective societies. Undoubtedly, all levels of government should be in service to their citizens. But, how do we get a good government?

Good politicians who provide successful leadership are perhaps the most important ingredients to an establishment and running of a good government, which provides the best possible services to its citizens.

---

[87] Paine, Thomas, *Of the Origin and Design of Government in General. With Concise Remarks on the English Constitution*, Philadelphia: February 14, 1776

Digging in a bit deeper, the question of how do we get good politicians comes up. In an attempt to respond to this question, let's recall a few major qualities that we believe are key attributes for a good politician – such as good character, clean personal history, acceptable personality, morale, strong leadership skills, organizational capacity, etc.

As any other post-communist and post-occupied state, Kosova too is striving to build a good state with a good government. But, to get a good government, Kosova needs good politicians. In light of Kosova's unique political circumstances, its strategic position in the heart of the Balkans, the increasing ambitions and efforts of the region's states to acquire EU membership, and the general globalization trend, this paper primarily looks at the changes in the lives of politicians in Kosova and how they will affect Kosova building of statehood in the next couple of decades.

## 2. A Brief Historical Note on Kosova

Kosova, an equally constituent part of the Yugoslavian Federation, was illegally and unwillingly stripped of its autonomous and constituent status within the Federation in 1989 by Belgrade, and as a result became one of the poorest and least developed parts of Yugoslavia, and even Europe. The decade of the 1990s marked a remarkable civil resistance of ethnic Albanians, who constitute over 90 % of Kosova's two million people, against the Serbian apartheid.

But, this civil resistance and the belief that the civilized world would come to support Kosova Albanians in their quest for freedom started to fade in the late 1990s. By 1997 armed guerilla Albanian groups emerged. The support for the armed resistance took a steep increase in 1998 when the Kosova Liberation Army (KLA) became publicly and officially the armed movement of Kosova Albanians fighting for freedom. The emergence of KLA triggered the Serb forces to undertake massive military offensives throughout Kosova during late 1998 and early 1999, resulting in mass murders and brutal expulsions. Such a grand-scale ethnic cleansing in the heart of Europe could no longer be  tolerated, bringing about NATO's intervention.

Until NATO's first war in the history of its existence, very few people knew where Kosova was or anything else about it.  However, scenes of brutality and genocide committed by Serbian forces against the ethnic

Albanian civilian population of Kosova shook the world in early 1999 and made Kosova a violently radiant place on the world map. To stop this unfolding "New Holocaust" — as many personalities familiar with the history of the Balkans and that of Kosova have put it — NATO engaged in a 79-day air strike campaign against Serbian forces.

Since NATO's successful military intervention, which resulted in all Serbian forces being withdrawn from Kosova, the country was put under the United Nations administration. According to the UNSC Resolution 1244 of 10 June 1999, the UN Mission in Kosova (UNMIK) was called upon to: perform basic civilian administrative functions; promote the establishment of substantial autonomy and self-government in Kosova; facilitate a political process to determine Kosova's future status; coordinate humanitarian and disaster relief of all international agencies; support the reconstruction of key infrastructure; maintain civil law and order; promote human rights; and assure the safe and unimpeded return of all refugees and displaced persons to their homes in Kosova. [88]

---

[88] United Nations Mission in Kosovo (official web-page: unmikonline.org)

However, UNMIK was neither mandated, nor sufficiently capable to assist Kosova in its much needed development effort. That is a task that was left to the European Union.

But, Kosova's economy was not only underdeveloped to begin with; it had also been harshly damaged for over a decade during the Serbian rule. As also noted by IMF, "the war provided a further setback to output and the quality and capacity of the infrastructure. Damage to the housing stock was particularly extensive, but the main utilities (power, telecommunications) also suffered considerable damage, as did some of the already dubiously viable industrial concerns."[89]

During the Serbian rule of the 1990s, Kosova Albanians were massively dismissed from public jobs. Being a socialist economy, most of the jobs in Kosova were in the public domain. So, this massive dismissal of Kosova Albanians created huge unemployment, which naturally fed into an increase in poverty. Being an Albanian in Kosova during the period of Serbian domination was an excuse not only to be dismissed from a job, but also to be

---

[89] Robert Corker, Dawn Rehm, Kristina Kostial, "Kosovo: Macroeconomic Issues and Fiscal Sustainability," IMF 2001

denied any public services — some as essential as health care and education.

Nevertheless, Kosova Albanians managed to establish a parallel state[90] run by a government-in-exile, which was successful in collecting voluntary, yet very significant amounts of money, into the Republic of Kosova Fund — named the "3 percent." This "3-percent" fund was mainly used to fund an underground education system and a quasi-public healthcare system. It also provided for a social welfare system to help those in extreme poverty.

Being a society with close family ties and very non-individualistic, Kosova Albanians in the diaspora played the most crucial role in ensuring the economic survival of the Albanians inside Kosova. Initially, only the diaspora members contributed into the "3-percent" fund. In addition, migrant Kosova Albanians, mainly residing in Western Europe, provided substantial financial assistance to their family, relatives, and friends in Kosova, especially over the decade of the 1990s.

---

[90] Howard Clark, *Civil Resistance in Kosovo*, Pluto Press: 2000

## 3. Kosova Politicians and its Statehood

The Kosova Albanian political class as an entity of its own emerged in 1989 with the establishment of the Kosova Democratic League (in Albanian: Lidhja Demokratike e Kosoves, LDK) led by Dr. Ibrahim Rugova, who successfully served as Kosova's leader until his loss of a short battle with cancer in January 2006. Most of its members came from the academic elites of Kosova. During the running of the so-called "Republic of Kosova" institutions (the parallel state) while under the Serbian rule, LDK served both as Kosova's national movement and its only political force. Elections were held, and a one-party government-in-exile was established.

Needless to say, the life of a typical Kosova politician during the 1990s consisted of repeated arrests, imprisonment, and even murder by the Serbian regime. Few were those wearing a politician's hat and not being persecuted by the Serbian regime.

But, with Kosova's liberation from Serbia in June 1999 came the blossom of a truly multi-party political system, and those wearing a politician's hat appeared like mushrooms after a healthy rain. Politicians now had a goal – power! Government power, as limited as it has been under UNMIK – which holds some executive powers such as defense, foreign affairs, finances – became the quest of Kosova politicians.

Since 1999, Kosova has successfully and democratically held two local elections (2000, 2002) and two national elections (2001, 2004).[91] In all four elections, LDK led by Dr. Rugova was an unbeatable party. While it did not win the absolute majority, it always ranked number one, sweeping in between 41 and 48 percent of Kosova's votes. The winning key – Dr. Rugova! Because he was the first and the only one to establish a political party and lead a national movement in Kosova in 1989 against all odds, given the Serbian regime brutality, the people simply adored him and believed in him.

With his passing, the political scene in Kosova has undoubtedly completely changed. LDK has split into two parties (LDK and LDD). The icon that people voted for forever is gone. This creates a lot of room for shifts in power. Still, LDK with a few smaller parties holds the major powers in a coalition government as a result of the 2004 national elections (which LDK had won because of Dr. Rugova).

Another crucial change that will soon take place in Kosova is the definition of its political status. Since June

---

[91] Kosovo Central Election Commission, http://internet.cec-ko.org/en/

1999, Kosova has been a UN protectorate administered by UNMIK and its own government. The Security Council is nowadays discussing a new resolution, which will endorse the Ahtisaari Plan[92] and grant Kosova full-fledged independence under the EU supervision for an interim period.

With the fight for independence a closed chapter within the next few months, the political scene in Kosova losses yet another important hook for votes. All of the parties in Kosova had independence as their number one priority and, of course, the parties with more international connections seemed more credible on the independence promise and thus won more votes.

Therefore, it will be very interesting to see how the politics in Kosova will play out in the next elections, which will be held after independence. More importantly, the question of the kind of government that Kosova will have and the kind of politicians that will make such a

---

[92] The Comprehensive Proposal for Kosovo Final Status Settlement is the final recommendation for Kosovo's future by the UN Special Envoy for Kosovo final status, Mr. Martti Ahtisaari, a former Finnish president, resulting from more than eighteen months of intense negations between Prishtina and Belgrade under the auspices of the UN. The Ahtisaari proposal provides for a "supervised independence" for Kosovo as a way to meet the Kosovo Albanian majority rightful demands, and a detailed decentralization plan to meet the Serbian minority demands. This proposal, backed by the US and EU, is now being debated at the UN Security Council and its approval—given Russia's non-use of veto—is expected to happen in June. The Kosovo National Assembly has already approved the Ahtisaari proposal in April, and thereby has committed to the implementation of its decentralization plan, among others.

government remains crucially important for Kosova's future as the newest state in Europe. Will the quest for Kosova as a European state now take prevalence among Kosova politicians? Will it be the case that the more Europeanized politicians will win more votes?

## 4. Determinants of Future Successful Politics in Kosova

Besides the EU membership card (given Kosova aspirations to join the Union), Kosova politicians will have to play wisely and strategically with a few other cards as well to be able to produce successful politics, and also successful policies resulting altogether in a successful state. Some of the other major cards include:

- *Assurance of support from the EU and the US:* A politician that will not have good connections within the EU and the US decision-making centers, and that will not be supported by them, is in no way ever going to succeed in Kosova politics. The majority of Kosovars (i.e. Albanians[93]) are the most pro-American and pro-Western people in the

---

[93] Serbs, who comprise about 10% of Kosovo's population, are mainly anti-American and anti-Western. This sentiment results from the NATO bombing against Serbia in 1999.

world.[94] To be able to ensure American and EU backing, a Kosova politician must insist on full implementation of the Ahtisaari Plan and the building of a multi-ethnic society in Kosova.

- *Continued national support:* But, EU and US are not going to vote in the Kosova elections. The Kosovars will. And, if a politician goes all the way to ensure US and EU support and publicly insists on making Kosova a multiethnic state (with only 10% minorities) along with full implementation of the Ahtisaari Plan, which calls for a particularly pro-Serb decentralization process, then he/she risks losing the majority support among ethnic Albanians.

- *Sound economic progress:* Economic progress is a must for Kosova to succeed as a state. Until independence, Kosova politicians could put the blame on the lack of statehood for bad economic performance. The future independent Kosova will no longer give them this option. Therefore, any aspiring politician must provide an implementable platform for economic prosperity. To ensure

---

[94] Pierre Hassner, "Beyond Iraq: The Transatlantic Crisis in Perspective," *IPRI*, Sep 30, 2004 (http://www.ipri.pt/artigos/artigo.php?ida=22)

economic development, Kosova must attract foreign direct investments – so, ties with potential foreign investors would be helpful.

At a more personal level, one to two decades from now, today's Kosova politicians will be finding themselves completely démodé. Most of Kosova's current political class hails from communist-trained and -educated elites. While they have modernized and transformed into democrats somewhat, their traits have not changed much. Kosova voters in the future will look for more inspiring and proven leadership suitable to the concerns and circumstances of the time. More importantly, Kosova's future voters will be the youth of today, who will eventually be well educated and speak more than one language.

Therefore, Kosova's future successful politicians will be the ones who dare to break away from the traditions of 'big promises politics' and winning votes on the basis of one iconographic individual or leader. They are to be upstanding people and fit for Kosova's future needs on their own.

More specifically, we could quite safely be able to characterize the future Kosova politicians who will hold offices in about one or two decades from now, in terms of Greenstein's characteristics of a politician in office.[95] Without picking on one single individual, in what follows, we will try to project what those characteristics that Greenstein provides are to look like for a politician to be successful in Kosova:

- *Political Communication:* A successful politician in Kosova must definitely be a very skilled political communicator to be able to ensure enough international support (from the EU and US mainly) and at the same time to avoid a negative backlash from the electorate (because of the obvious tension between Kosovars and the international community as far as the full implementation of the Ahtisaari Plan and Kosova's definition as a multiethnic state are concerned)

- *Organizational Capacity:* This is always a good asset to have. But, if surrounded by a greatly professional and well-organized team, one can get away easily without much organizational capacity. In the case of Kosova, this presents a drastic change for future generations of leaders – they are

[95] Fred I. Greenstein, *The Presidential Difference: Leadership Style From FDR to George W. Bush*, Little Brown, Boston: 2004

to either be very organizationally capable themselves (which is rarely the case) or be surrounded by professional and qualified people, which has not happened so far – today's politicians tend to have less qualified people on their staffs as a result of family nepotism, political favors, etc.

- *Political Skill:* This is very necessary to make sure Kosova survives and progresses beyond the wounds of its war-time past. It also helps with making sure each citizen of Kosova will come to respect its institutions regardless of their ethnicity, religion, etc. It helps ensure a more compact state with equal rights for all.

- *Vision:* No doubt that having a clear and implementable vision for Kosova as an EU member will be key to becoming a successful politician in Kosova. However, given the past visionary, but empty, promises of Kosova politicians, the future generation will be more carefully weighing a politician's vision between what can be turned into reality and what is likely to remain only a dream.

- *Cognitive Style:* Until now, usually the well connected among parties came to power, regardless of their own abilities or wisdom. The future electorate will no longer tolerate this. Open-list voting, which is expected to increase personal accountability for politicians, will actually be implemented in post-independence elections. Therefore, no longer will a wanna-be politician be able to come to power without a firm personal foundation of achievements.

- *Emotional Intelligence:* This will perhaps be a key factor to a politician's ability to maintain the support of the Albanian majority and at the same time win the institutional respect at least, if not the support, of the Serbian minority. A successful Kosova politician that has this ability will likely be able to ensure a faster and safer pace of prosperity for the country as a whole.

While it is almost clear that Kosova will earn independence and be a state of its own, what only the future will tell is whether Kosova will be a European state or a just another state in Europe. As we all hope for Kosova to succeed as a democratic state, it is clear that the burden for Kosova as a European state falls upon its future generations of both voters and politicians. Only politicians that are upstanding, fit for Kosova's future needs, meet the descriptions listed above in terms of their characteristics at a personal level, and strategically fall within the determinants of successful politics will tremendously help in ensuring that Kosova becomes a truly European state and not just a failed state in Europe.

# Bibliography

Howard Clark, *Civil Resistance in Kosovo*, Pluto Press: 2000

Robert Corker, Dawn Rehm, Kristina Kostial, "Kosovo: Macroeconomic Issues and Fiscal Sustainability," IMF 2001

Fred I. Greenstein, *The Presidential Difference: Leadership Style From FDR to George W. Bush*, Little Brown, Boston: 2004

Pierre Hassner, "Beyond Iraq: The Transatlantic Crisis in Perspective," *IPRI*, Sep 30, 2004 (http://www.ipri.pt/artigos/artigo.php?ida=22)

Thomas Paine, *Of the Origin and Design of Government in General. With Concise Remarks on the English Constitution*, Philadelphia: February 14, 1776

Kosovo Central Election Commission, http://internet.cec-ko.org/en/

United Nations Mission in Kosovo (official web-page: unmikonline.org)

# Are They Kosova Serbs or the Riches of Trepça that Serbia Cares More About?

# Are They Kosova Serbs or the Riches of Trepça that Serbia Cares More About?

## 1. Introduction

The UN Security Council is nowadays discussing a new resolution, which will have to endorse the Ahtisaari Plan[96] and grant Kosova independence under the EU supervision for an interim period, after over eight years of UN protectorate. While for Serbia, independence remains unacceptable, the reasons for such flat denial of an outcome that most of the world has come to endorse are not as clear.

---

[96] The Comprehensive Proposal for Kosovo Final Status Settlement is the final recommendation for Kosovo's future by the UN Special Envoy for Kosovo final status, Mr. Martti Ahtisaari, a former Finnish president, resulting from more than eighteen months of intense negations between Prishtina and Belgrade under the auspices of the UN. The Ahtisaari proposal provides for a "supervised independence" for Kosovo as a way to meet the Kosovo Albanian majority rightful demands, and a detailed decentralization plan to meet the Serbian minority demands. This proposal, backed by the US and EU, is now being debated at the UN Security Council and its approval—given Russia's non-use of veto—is expected to happen in June. The Kosovo National Assembly has already approved the Ahtisaari proposal in April, and thereby has committed to the implementation of its decentralization plan, among others.

Serbia's insistence on a full-fledged decentralization plan (which requires more authority for Serb-majority municipalities in Kosova and a special status for the Northern Kosova region which is mostly Serb-inhabited that what the Ahtisaari Plan envisions), may not only come from its caring for the Serbian minority rights in a new independent Albanian-led Kosova, but also from its greater and deeper interests of economic nature strictly related to Northern Kosova, namely the Trepca (original spelling: *Trepça*) mines.

The riches of Trepca are not a secret. Its crystals, for instance, are very much valued and extremely rare. Some of Trepca crystals are proudly exhibited at some of the world's most famous museums.[97] The Trepca mines are exceptionally rich with zinc, lead, other metals, and less so with gold and silver as well.[98]

Trepca mines happen to be located in the Northern Kosova, nearby the still ethnically divided town of Mitrovica, and the majority of population of that part is Serbian. The fact that Serbs populate this region of Kosova has, therefore, served as an excuse for Serbia to insist on a very extensive decentralization plan and even a special

---

[97] George Kosich, "A look back at Kosovo's Trecpa mines," *SerbWorld USA*, Vol. XV, No. 6, July/August 1999 (http://www.serbworldusa.com/TREPCA.html)

[98] Ministry of Energy and Mines of Kosovo (www.mem-ks.com)

status for Northern Kosova. While the claim that Serbia wants special autonomous status of Northern Kosova, led by local Serbs, if Kosova ultimately gets independent, has not been publicly and widely made, it is crucial to understand that when it has much to do with Serbia's thirst for Trepca riches and very little with its caring of the Serbian minority within an independent Kosova.

Because the importance of Trepca goes beyond its economic impact—it also has political implications—this paper primarily looks at the significance of Trepca in the final stages of determining Kosova's final status over the next few months. For a better understanding of the Kosova issue, we will give a brief introduction of Kosova's past and present and then provide an analysis of Trepca's history and the reasons as to why Serbia's insistence of holding some control over at least Northern Kosova by all costs is so pungent. We end by providing a few policy recommendations that could help make Trepca a leading mine in the region.

## 2. A Brief Historical Note on Kosova

Kosova, an equally constituent part of the Yugoslavian Federation, was illegally and unwillingly stripped of its autonomous and constituent status within the Federation in 1989 by Belgrade, and as a result became one of the poorest and least developed parts of Yugoslavia, and even Europe. The decade of the 1990s marked a remarkable civil resistance of ethnic Albanians, who constitute over 90% of Kosova's two million people, against the Serbian apartheid.

But, this civil resistance and the belief that the civilized world would come to support Kosova Albanians in their quest for freedom started to fade in the late 1990s. By 1997 armed guerilla Albanian groups emerged. The support for the armed resistance took a steep increase in 1998 when the Kosova Liberation Army (KLA) became publicly and officially the armed movement of Kosova Albanians fighting for freedom. The emergence of KLA triggered the Serb forces to undertake massive military offensives throughout Kosova during late 1998 and early 1999, resulting in mass murders and brutal expulsions. Such a grand-scale ethnic cleansing in the heart of Europe could no longer be tolerated, bringing about NATO's intervention.

Until NATO's first war in the history of its existence, very few people knew where Kosova was or anything else about it. However, scenes of brutality and genocide committed by Serbian forces against the ethnic Albanian civilian population of Kosova shook the world in early 1999 and made Kosova a violently radiant place on the world map. To stop this unfolding "New Holocaust" — as many personalities familiar with the history of the Balkans and that of Kosova have put it — NATO engaged in a 79-day air strike campaign against Serbian forces.

Since NATO's successful military intervention, which resulted in all Serbian forces being withdrawn from Kosova, the country was put under the United Nations administration. According to the UNSC Resolution 1244 of 10 June 1999, the UN Mission in Kosova (UNMIK) was called upon to: perform basic civilian administrative functions; promote the establishment of substantial autonomy and self-government in Kosova; facilitate a political process to determine Kosova's future status; coordinate humanitarian and disaster relief of all international agencies; support the reconstruction of key infrastructure; maintain civil law and order; promote human rights; and assure the safe and unimpeded return of all refugees and displaced persons to their homes in Kosova. [99]

---

[99] United Nations Mission in Kosovo (official web-page: unmikonline.org)

However, UNMIK was neither mandated, nor sufficiently capable to assist Kosova in its much needed development effort. That is a task that was left to the European Union.

But, Kosova's economy was not only underdeveloped to begin with; it had also been harshly damaged for over a decade during the Serbian rule. As also noted by IMF, "the war provided a further setback to output and the quality and capacity of the infrastructure. Damage to the housing stock was particularly extensive, but the main utilities (power, telecommunications) also suffered considerable damage, as did some of the already dubiously viable industrial concerns."[100]

During the Serbian rule of the 1990s, Kosova Albanians were massively dismissed from public jobs. Being a socialist economy, most of the jobs in Kosova were in the public domain. So, this massive dismissal of Kosova Albanians created huge unemployment, which naturally fed into an increase in poverty. Being an Albanian in Kosova during the period of Serbian domination was an excuse not only to be dismissed from a job, but also to be

---

[100] Robert Corker, Dawn Rehm, Kristina Kostial, "Kosovo: Macroeconomic Issues and Fiscal Sustainability," IMF 2001

denied any public services—some as essential as health care and education.

Nevertheless, Kosova Albanians managed to establish a parallel state[101] run by a government-in-exile, which was successful in collecting voluntary, yet very significant amounts of money, into the Republic of Kosova Fund—named the "3 percent." This "3-percent" fund was mainly used to fund an underground education system and a quasi-public healthcare system. It also provided for a social welfare system to help those in extreme poverty.

Being a society with close family ties and very non-individualistic, Kosova Albanians in the diaspora played the most crucial role in ensuring the economic survival of the Albanians inside Kosova. Initially, only the diaspora members contributed into the "3-percent" fund. In addition, migrant Kosova Albanians, mainly residing in Western Europe, provided substantial financial assistance to their family, relatives, and friends in Kosova, especially over the decade of the 1990s.

## 3. The Trepca Mines of Kosova

Trepca, besides its economic significance, is also one of the symbols of Kosova Albanians' struggle against

---

[101] Howard Clark, *Civil Resistance in Kosovo*, Pluto Press: 2000

the Miloshevic-era Serb regime of the 1990s. The Albanian miners at Trepca were one of the first to publicly denounce the Miloshevic's regime by entering a hunger strike some 600 meters below surface.[102] This strike, which took place in 1987 and lasted for several days, gave a very strong a clear signal to Belgrade that Kosova Albanians were serious about their demands for equality and statehood within the then-Yugoslav Federation.

For a better introduction of the Trepca Mines, we turn to a report by the International Crisis Group on Trepca, which is one of the very few comprehensive studies on Trepca's history. Trepca Mines, "conglomerate of some 40 mines and factories, located mostly in Kosova but also in other locations in Serbia and Montenegro. Its activities include chemical processing and production of goods as varied as batteries and paint. But the heart of its operations, and the source of most of its raw material, is the vast mining complex to the east of Mitrovicë/a in the north of Kosova, famous since Roman times."[103]

The importance of Trepca, both in economic and political terms, is asserted in this ICG report as well – "The future of Trepca cuts to the heart of the Kosovars' identity.

---

[102] Michael Palairet, "Trepca, 1965-2000," *EU Pillar of UNMIK*, Prishtina: 2000

[103] *Trepca: Making Sense of the Labyrinth*, IGC Report 26 November 1999

Its great mineral wealth is the basis of the economy of Kosova, but the complex is badly run-down as a result of under-investment and over-exploitation by governments in Belgrade."[104] While Kosova was under the Serbian regime, Belgrade massively over-exploited Trepca and misused most of its profits. As a result, the phrase *"Trepca se radi, Novi Beograd se gradi,"* which means *"Trepca works, New Belgrade builds,"* became famous among all of the then-Yugoslavia, and especially during the late 1970s and 1980s. This anecdotal expression clearly conveys the message of Trepca's profits' misuse by Belgrade. Instead of investing some of the profits into new technology and better infrastructure for the complex or for other public goods in Kosova, the Serbian management sent almost all of the profit into Serbia proper.

To make this point more vivid, the ICG report says that "from 1981-89, Belgrade monopolized the export of Trepca's minerals to Russia and elsewhere, reaping the profits in hard currency and oil, while compensating the Kosovars only with electricity and other non-fungible forms of payment." Because, Kosova Albanians treasured Trepca and understood that investment in the complex were needed for further progress, the Kosova Albanian

---

[104] ibid.

management "attempted to sell its products on the European market and to modernize the facilities' modes of production, only to be foiled time and again by the Serbian government, which was in the process of "integrating" Serbia's economy - that is, of tethering all economic sectors even more closely to Belgrade."[105]

With the expulsion of Kosova Albanians from their jobs at Trepca, and due to the lack of their expertise, most of Trepca plants closed during the early 1990.[106] Nevertheless, after several years of harsh sanctions instituted by the international community as punishment for Belgrade's role in the Bosnian war, "Belgrade was looking for ways to acquire large injections of cash,"[107] and quickly decided that exploiting Trepca was its only option. According to some Serbian official sources that the ICG report draws from, only in 1996, Belgrade ended up making about $100 million in Trepca exports, making Trepca thus the largest exporting company in the Yugoslav Federation.

Therefore, this brief introductory analysis of Trepca Mines points to why Serbia would want to keep control over Trepca. After all, its riches are clearly

---

[105] *Trepca: Making Sense of the Labyrinth*, IGC Report 26 November 1999

[106] Noel Malcolm, *Kosovo: A Short History*, NYU Press, New York: July 1999

[107] *Trepca: Making Sense of the Labyrinth*, IGC Report 26 November 1999

something of benefit for Serbia. If working properly and at full capacity, Trepca may again be the source out of which Serbia may get the revenues it so desperately needs to develop its economy and infrastructure, which was heavily damaged during the NATO bombing campaign of 1999.

As for the Kosova Albanians, it is crucial for Trepca to start operating as soon as possible. The Trepca complex was shut down after Kosova became a UN protectorate in June 1999. According to UNMIK Regulation 1999/1, all publicly- and socially-owned enterprises and properties in the territory of Kosova came under the direct control of UNMIK.[108] Because Trepca's status as a socially owned enterprise, it automatically fell under the UNMIK management. After a feasibility study, UNMIK decided to completely shut down Trepca in 2000 due to the lack of proper safety measures for safe mining, old and defective technology, and lack environmentally protective equipment.[109]

Even after the shut down, the Serbian government kept insisting that Trepca is crucial for its economy and should be allowed to operate. Belgrade went as far as to

---

[108] UNMIK Regulation 1999/1, The UNMIK Official Gazette (www.unmikonline.org)

[109] Kosovo Economic News, *EU Pillar of UNMIK*, Prishtina: 2000

supposedly fraudulently present some foreign mining consortiums – such as Société Commerciale de Métaux et de Minéraux (SCMM), a Paris-based firm, and Mytilineos Holdings S.A., an Athens-based firm – as legal shareholders of Trepca.[110] Belgrade hoped that through foreign consortiums being presented as shareholders of Trepca, it could get UNMIK to allow for Trepca's operation under Belgrade's control.

From a Kosova Albanian perspective, Trepca is seen as the number one locomotive of Kosova's economic drive. They believe that if Trepca becomes fully operational, then the unemployment rate, which currently stands at staggering high levels between 40-60%,[111] would eventually go down. Given the Trepca complex vast operation and production units, which at its peak production periods employed as many as 15,000 people,[112] it is reasonable then for Kosova to insist in Trepca's quick revitalization in light of the high unemployment rate and the fact that about half of Kosova's population is under the age of 25.[113]

---

[110] *Trepca: Making Sense of the Labyrinth*, IGC Report 26 November 1999

[111] *Kosovo in Figures 2005*, Statistical Office of Kosovo, Prishtina: 2006

[112] Michael Palairet, "Trepca, 1965-2000," *EU Pillar of UNMIK*, Prishtina: 2000

[113] *Kosovo in Figures 2005*, Statistical Office of Kosovo, Prishtina: 2006

Besides it economic impact on Kosova's society, the Kosova Albanians, as stated earlier, see Trepca also as a symbol of their national resistance against the Serbian regime. In this context, the Kosova government insists on a plan for sustainable operation and step-by-step modernization and full recovery of the Trepca complex. The revitalization of the Trepca complex is listed as one of the priorities of the Kosova's government Ministry of Energy and Mines.[114] A similar view is held in the ICG report, too, which states that it is very important for Kosovars to see some signs of progress towards some degree of economic normality and prosperity and that "the return to work of even a few hundred Kosovar miners would represent, for all Kosovars, the reclaiming of their patrimony"[115] and this process must be adequately supported and facilitated by the international community and UNMIK, which would also show that Trepca's symbolic and economic importance for Kosova is respected.

---

[114] Ministry of Energy and Mines of Kosovo, Overview of Kosovo's Mines (www.mem-ks.com)

[115] *Trepca: Making Sense of the Labyrinth*, IGC Report 26 November 1999

# 4. What's Really at Stake for Serbia?

When Serbia insists on a particularly pro-Serb decentralization for Kosova, which would enable Serb-run municipalities to associate among themselves and with the state of Serbia, and to have full control over their own local affairs as far as economic development, healthcare, education, and police are concerned,[116] one cannot but think about what is really at stake for Serbia here?

Belgrade knows that Kosova will never come under its rule again. This point has been repeatedly made clear by senior international diplomats and even the Contact Group.[117] Furthermore, the recent Ahtisaari Plan for the settlement of Kosova's final status, which has been endorsed by the West and the UN Secretary General, and is now being debated at the UN Security Council and is expected to be approved by a formal resolution, clearly cuts off every single remaining formal connection between Kosova and Serbia by granting Kosova independence, supervised by the EU for an interim period.[118]

---

[116] "Serbia Calls for 'Meaningful Decentralization,'" Kosova Information Center, March 2007 (www.kosova.com)

[117] Ten Guideline Principles for Resolving the Kosovo Status, The Contact Group, London: October 7, 2005

[118] Martti Ahtisaari, "The Comprehensive Proposal for Kosovo Final Status Settlement," UNOSEK, Vienna: March 2007

Despite this truth, Serbia keeps playing the card of its "constitutional obligation" to protect the Serbian minority within Kosova. Given that it will not succeed in keeping its sovereignty over Kosova any longer, Belgrade now wants to at least get something valuable out of this "loss," as it refers to Kosova's becoming independent.

The riches of Trepca and the prospects of turning it into a cash-cow one more time to benefit Serbia is what really Serbia is going after now – by insisting on a decentralization plan that empowers local Serbs to have control over their local affairs (including economic development). Serbia really does not care much about the rights of the Kosova Serbs. If it really cared, then it would call upon the Serbs in Kosova to fully participate in the Kosova institutions and not to boycott them.[119] After all, Kosova is a democracy and minority rights can be best ensured through full participation of these minorities in the institutions of the country.

Therefore, Belgrade wants to keep control of Trepca by all means possible. The two cards being currently played through which Belgrade is hoping to remain in control of Trepca are decentralization and some

---

[119] "Koshtunica: Serbs to Boycott Kosovo Elections," Kosova Information Center, September 2004 (www.kosova.com)

sort of a special autonomous status for Northern Kosova. If decentralization were to happen as per Belgrade's demands, then indeed Kosova would find itself in a very unfavorable position as far as managing of Trepca is concerned. In an ala-Belgrade decentralization, Serb municipalities of northern Kosova would have the ability and the power to connect to Belgrade directly and work with it on important economic issues. Given that most of Trepca operation and production units and mines are in the northern Kosova and fall under the jurisdiction of the northern Serbian municipalities, then Belgrade would be able to remain in control of Trepca through these municipalities. While the Serbian politicians would not admit the fact that their insistence on such a crazy decentralization plan hides behind their desire to control Trepca, others sometimes make similar claims quite openly.[120]

The scenario of granting the northern Serbs a special "autonomous status" within an independent Kosova, which has also been brought up as an option that would lure Serbia into recognizing Kosova's

[120] Diane Johnstone, "How it is done – Taking over the Trepca mines: Plans and Propaganda," *The Emperor's New Clothes*, February 2000
(http://www.tenc.net/articles/Johnstone/howitis.htm)

independence,[121] and which Serbia will play as its last card right before the final approval of the Ahtisaari Plan by the UN Security Council, also would grant Belgrade some sort of control over the riches of Trepca.

While the decentralization plan envisioned in the Ahtisaari Plan has not, fortunately, met all of the Belgrade's demands, the card on special "autonomous status" for northern Kosova Serbs is what Belgrade is now using to try to prevent or at least modify the Ahtisaari Plan before the UN Security Council approves it. Russia has been an enormous support for Belgrade in this regard, as it is the only veto-powered UNSC member that has not yet endorsed the Ahtisaari Plan. But, even though Belgrade is probably trying to get this call for an "autonomous status" for northern Kosova Serbs to become part of the Ahtisaari Plan behind closed doors through Russia, its efforts will most likely fail given the strong backing of the Ahtisaari Plan as is by the US, EU and other UNSC countries.

The bottom line, however, remains that Belgrade's demands for so-called "protection of its people within Kosova," are really just political statements which are

---

[121] Charles A. Kupchan, "Independence for Kosovo," *Foreign Affairs*, November/December 2005

better acceptable internationally. The true reasons behind Serbia's insistence of Serbs having major powers over their local districts, nevertheless, have much more to do with its ambitions to control Trepca.

## 5. Recommendations: What Next?

It is very likely that the UN Security Council will approve the Ahtisaari Plan in its current form. While the Plan gives Kosova Serbs a high degree of local powers over their municipalities, it clearly subjects them to Kosova national laws and central institutions of government. As such, the Plan does not give Serbia any particular treatment as far as Kosova internal issues are concerned — thus, making it impossible for Serbia to have any control over what it wants most – Trepca.

As for Trepca itself, the following is a list of recommendations that may help its recovery in the best interest of Kosova in the short run:

- A short-term strategy should be put in place by the Kosova government to revitalize at least key production units of the Trepca complex immediately;

- International technical and financial support must be sought in an effort to modernize the technology of Trepca;

- The Trepca complex should be considered of special national interest for Kosova and it should only be privatized when public management deems inappropriate and economically unsustainable;

- Any outstanding Trepca debts are to be borne by its previous masters – namely, Belgrade

- Any claims of investment in Trepca by Belgrade are baseless and can be countered-weighted by the profits that Belgrade alone extracted from Trepca;

- A special Trepca Board should be set up – consisting of government appointees, civil society professionals, and former Trepca management members – to manage Trepca until its future fate is decided at the appropriate time.

# Bibliography

Martti Ahtisaari, "The Comprehensive Proposal for Kosovo Final Status Settlement," UNOSEK, Vienna: March 2007

Howard Clark, *Civil Resistance in Kosovo*, Pluto Press: 2000

Robert Corker, Dawn Rehm, Kristina Kostial, "Kosovo: Macroeconomic Issues and Fiscal Sustainability," IMF 2001

Diane Johnstone, "How it is done – Taking over the Trepca mines: Plans and Propaganda," *The Emperor's New Clothes*, February 2000 (http://www.tenc.net/articles/Johnstone/howitis.htm)

George Kosich, "A look back at Kosovo's Trecpa mines," *SerbWorld USA*, Vol. XV, No. 6, July/August 1999 (http://www.serbworldusa.com/TREPCA.html)

Kosovo Economic News, *EU Pillar of UNMIK*, Prishtina: 2000

*Kosovo in Figures 2005*, Statistical Office of Kosovo, Prishtina: 2006

"Koshtunica: Serbs to Boycott Kosovo Elections," Kosova Information Center, September 2004 (www.kosova.com)

Charles A. Kupchan, "Independence for Kosovo," *Foreign Affairs*, November/December 2005

Noel Malcolm, *Kosovo: A Short History*, NYU Press, New York: July 1999

Ministry of Energy and Mines of Kosovo (www.mem-ks.com)

Ministry of Energy and Mines of Kosovo, Overview of Kosovo's Mines (www.mem-ks.com)

Michael Palairet, "Trepca, 1965-2000," *EU Pillar of UNMIK*, Prishtina: 2000

"Serbia Calls for 'Meaningful Decentralization,'" Kosova Information Center, March 2007 (www.kosova.com)

*Trepca: Making Sense of the Labyrinth*, IGC Report 26 November 1999

Ten Guideline Principles for Resolving the Kosovo Status, The Contact Group, London: October 7, 2005

United Nations Mission in Kosovo (official web-page: unmikonline.org)

UNMIK Regulation 1999/1, The UNMIK Official Gazette (www.unmikonline.org)

# DEMOGRAPHICS AND MIGRATION:
## Kosova's Private Sector Development at Crossroads

# Demographics and Migration:
## *Kosova's Private Sector Development at Crossroads*

A former communist economy and worn out society because of its recent ethnic conflict, Kosova remains a challenge not only in the field of economic development, but also in that of political status definition in the hands of the international community. Prior to Kosova's becoming an international protectorate under the United Nations, most of its industries have, of course, been under the control of the state and run by the state. Public and social enterprises have been the major economic drivers in Kosova just like in the rest of the region during the socialist era of the 1980s and 1990s.

Private sector development has been seen as an important component of Kosova's overall desired economic growth since UN took over in June 1999.

Privatization of POEs and SOEs[122] became a major undertaking of the European Union-led efforts to promote economic growth in Kosova. While over twenty-five waves of privatization have so far taken place, much remains to be done before most of these privatized SOEs and POEs start to normally function in a productive way.

Beyond privatization, series of micro-finance programs and institutions have been established in Kosova (such as Kosova Enterprise Program, FINCA, etc.) all in an attempt to help private sector development. Yet, Kosova suffers from a hugely underdeveloped economy and incredibly high unemployment, ranging between 40-60%, depending on the source.[123] With a population of about two million, half of which is under the age of 25,[124] Kosova is now at a very important stage in its demographic development. Given Europe's rapidly aging population, young people are one of the most valuable resources Kosova has. It may well be said that Kosova in about ten to fifteen years from now will be at

---

[122] POE – Privately Owned Enterprise; SOE – Socially Owned Enterprise

[123] Official statistics show unemployment at 39.7% (Statistical Office of Kosova, *Kosova in Figures 2005*),
while many other articles and studies claim the rate of unemployment at about 60%.

[124] Kosova in Figures 2005, *Statistical Office of Kosova*, Prishtina, 2006

the peak of its "demographic window of opportunity,"[125] which represents the best demographic stage for a country's rapid economic progress, given the fact that the labour-inactive and elderly people will only comprise a small percentage of the overall population, whereas the majority will be labour-active, young capable adults. Taking advantage of this demographic window of opportunity has been a major contributor to several emerging Asian countries' economic growth.[126]

Normally, one would expect that just like some Asian countries, Kosova could too take advantage of its young population when at its peak of the demographic window of opportunity to reach a miracle in economic development. One way to achieve this would be through incentives and programmes that would first enable these young Kosovars become well educated and well trained for the global economy of the twenty-first century and second, create opportunities for their entrepreneurship to be successful – hence, private sector development is the most efficient and sustainable way to not only accommodate such a labour force but to also give it room for further continued growth.

[125] Bloom, D.E., Williamson, J.G. "Demographic Transitions and Economic Miracles in Emerging Asia," *NBER Working Paper No. W6268*, November 1997
[126] Ibid.

Proving quality education for Kosova's youth is essential. But, it alone does not guarantee job growth. You simply need both demand and supply. Kosova, for obvious reasons, cannot compete in labour-intensive manufacturing with China or India for instance, but it can be a strategic source of relatively good quality products and mainly services for its reach European neighbours. To become attractive to the EU market, Kosova must have a quality educated labour force. To make this labour force active, Kosova must have fairly well developed free enterprises with a global and especially European outlook. Such enterprises may come into life only when private sector in Kosova is both strong and sustainable. Some may argue that developing the private sector (which would be attractive to / require educated professionals) in and of itself needs such professionals to begin with, and as a result this entire strategy seems as a "catch twenty-two." But, this kind of an analogy here is flawed because quality education of Kosova's young population, just like in other developing countries, must be of elementary focus for general development purposes and as such, it may then only be followed by the development of a particular sector – such as the private sector in this case.

Even though, Kosova may have the advantage of approaching its demographic window of opportunity, which may be well utilized to promote economic growth through private sector development, it faces another quite significant problem – migration. Historically, Kosova has been dependent on remittances, which in given particular times of its past, have been a lifeline for Kosovars.[127] Even today, a vast majority of young Kosovars want to immigrate usually to Western European and North American countries. They see no prospective in their own country. And, the ones who stay here are usually not much enthusiastic about getting educated. Contributing to this mind-set of young Kosovars has been the regular inflow of remittances. Kosova represents one of the top twenty countries in the world with the highest amount of remittances as share of GDP.

[127] "Cutting the Lifeline: Migration, Families and the Future of Kosova", *European Stability Initiative*, Berlin September 2006

**Figure 1: Top Twenty Remittance-Recipient Countries as Share of GDP**

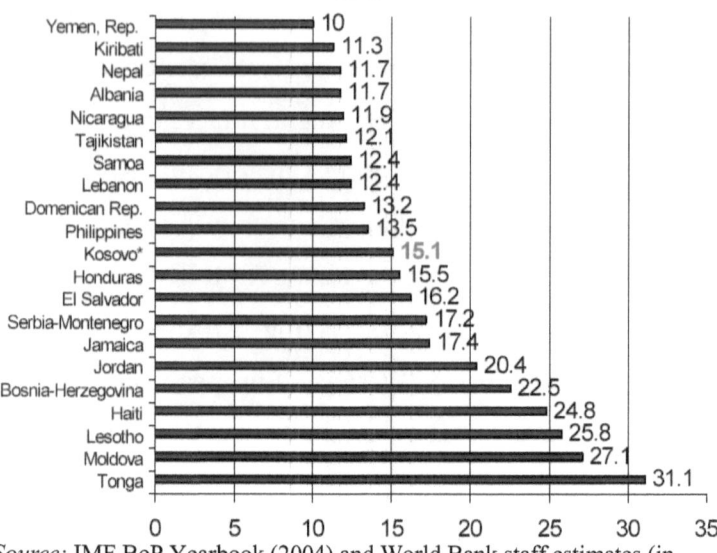

|  |  |
|---|---|
| Yemen, Rep. | 10 |
| Kiribati | 11.3 |
| Nepal | 11.7 |
| Albania | 11.7 |
| Nicaragua | 11.9 |
| Tajikistan | 12.1 |
| Samoa | 12.4 |
| Lebanon | 12.4 |
| Domenican Rep. | 13.2 |
| Philippines | 13.5 |
| Kosovo* | 15.1 |
| Honduras | 15.5 |
| El Salvador | 16.2 |
| Serbia-Montenegro | 17.2 |
| Jamaica | 17.4 |
| Jordan | 20.4 |
| Bosnia-Herzegovina | 22.5 |
| Haiti | 24.8 |
| Lesotho | 25.8 |
| Moldova | 27.1 |
| Tonga | 31.1 |

*Source:* IMF BoP Yearbook (2004) and World Bank staff estimates (in GEP 2006)

Generally studies have shown indications that remittances help reduce poverty. A study of 71 developing countries, for instance, showed that a 10 percent increase in per capita official international remittances led to a 3.5 percent decline in the share of people living in poverty.[128] As for Kosova, however, it has been shown that while remittances have generally helped the consumption needs of recipients, they have also had a negative impact on

---

[128] Adams, Richard and John Page, "Do International Migration and Remittances Reduce Poverty in Developing Countries?" *World Development* 33(10): 1645–69, 2005

young recipients as far as their education attainment and labour force participation are concerned.[129]    Remittances (from family members and others abroad, including foreign pensions) constitute the second largest source of income for households in Kosova, making up about 16% of household income.

**Table 1: Household Income Sources in Kosova (% of total income)**

| Income Source | Men | Women | All |
|---|---|---|---|
| Regular Wages | 51 | 58 | 51 |
| Temporary Wages | 7 | 1 | 6 |
| Business Net | 11 | 1 | 9 |
| Agriculture Net | 3 | 1 | 6 |
| From members abroad | 9 | 12 | 10 |
| From others abroad | 3 | 3 | 3 |
| Kosovo Pensions | 3 | 15 | 5 |
| Pensions from abroad | 3 | 2 | 3 |
| Remitt's from Kosovo | 1 | 1 | 1 |
| Property Income | 2 | 1 | 2 |
| Social Welfare | 2 | 3 | 3 |
| Lotteries | 0 | 0 | 0 |
| Other | 2 | 1 | 2 |
| Wages in kind | 1 | 1 | 1 |
| In kind from abroad | 0 | 0 | 0 |
| Total % | 100 | 100 | 100 |

*Source:* Statistical Office of Kosova (2006)

[129] Bislimi, Faton and Ersegun Kayhan, "The Spoil Effect: How Remittances Affect Developing Countries – The Case of Kosova," *MPAID Second Year Policy Analysis Series*, John F. Kennedy School of Government, Harvard University, March 2007

So, while young population is one of Kosova's major resources for progress, and while the private sector development could be the way to take advantage of its demographic window of opportunity, keeping this resource in and active is particularly challenging because of the negative effects on education and labour-force participation that remittances have on their recipients and the fact that these young people want to immigrate. This challenge brings private sector development in Kosova at the crossroads of migration and demographics.

Therefore, it is of outmost importance for Kosova policymakers to rightly decide on a policy or a set of policies that encourage education attainment and discourage further immigration of its young people. To be successful, these policies should not only be technically right, but they should also be politically supportable as well as practically implementable. One recommendation to be considered would be for Kosova to perhaps establish and develop an investment bank that would attract the savings and other financial transactions of the Kosova diaspora (by of course providing slightly higher interest rates than the average EU commercial banks given Kosova's higher risk level, or by providing social and other financial benefits – such as reimbursement of taxation from saving accounts earnings when these funds are invested in Kosova, for instance). Such a bank, if pursuing policies in line with the above, could be instrumental in helping all of the components of economic growth through private sector development fall into their right places, because:

- it would enable Kosovar migrants to seriously consider having their funds saved and invested in Kosova (which would create a more sustainable source of income for Kosovars in general, and their family and relatives in particular) as opposed to sending them in the form of remittances used mainly for consumption by their family and relatives in Kosova;

- it would signal Kosovar youths that their country is rather seen as a potential place for investment (which would in turn create new jobs in the future), which would decrease their ambition to leave Kosova and increase their ambition for higher education attainment;

- it would finally provide Kosova with the point where both the supply and demand in terms of its demographic window of opportunity and the investment for private entrepreneurship progress, respectively, would meet – hence, taking advantage of both demographics and migration to ensure economic growth through private sector development.

# *Bibliography*

Adams, Richard and John Page, "Do International Migration and Remittances Reduce Poverty in Developing Countries?" *World Development* 33(10): 1645–69, 2005

Bislimi, Faton and Ersegun Kayhan, "The Spoil Effect: How Remittances Affect Developing Countries – The Case of Kosova," *MPAID Second Year Policy Analysis Series*, John F. Kennedy School of Government, Harvard University, March 2007

Bloom, D.E., Williamson, J.G. "Demographic Transitions and Economic Miracles in
Emerging Asia," *NBER Working Paper No. W6268*, November 1997

"Cutting the Lifeline: Migration, Families and the Future of Kosova", *European Stability Initiative*, Berlin September 2006

Kosova in Figures 2005, *Statistical Office of Kosova*, Prishtina, 2006

# KOSOVA EMIGRATION TRENDS

# Kosova Emigration Trends

The diaspora has always been an important part of Kosova's society, not only in terms of financial support, but also in terms of social life. Financially speaking, remittances and pensions from abroad form a significant source of income for Kosovans in general, and K-Albanians in particular. Almost €400 million have come into Kosova in the form of remittances in 2007[130].

Nevertheless, the general public belief is that Kosovans want to emigrate mainly for economic reasons. The following is a very brief descriptive analysis of Kosova's emigration trends based on the October 2007 Early Warning System (EWS) opinion poll results, which reveals some insightful information.

According to the poll, more than one-third of K-Albanians and Other minorities and some 18% of K-Serbs reported to have a family member abroad, while the majority of all ethnicities in Kosova reported to have no family member abroad. It must be noted, however, that

---

[130] CBAK, October 2007 Statistics Bulletin

by family member the questionnaire identified immediate family members such as father, mother, wife, brother, sister, son, or daughter.

**Table 1: Do you have any family members living abroad?**

| | | Ethnicity | |
| | K-Albanian | K-Serb | Others |
| --- | --- | --- | --- |
| Yes | 32.0% | 17.5% | 30.0% |
| No | 67.3% | 75.6% | 70.0% |
| DK/NA | 0.7% | 6.8% | |
| Total | 100.0% | 100.0% | 100.0% |

DK/NA – Don't Know / No Answer

Out of those with family members abroad, the vast majority of K-Albanians (82%) stated that they receive financial support from their family members abroad occasionally and on a regular basis, while only 16% stated that they do not receive any financial support. The trend is quite opposite for K-Serbs, only 14% of whom stated that they receive financial support from their family members abroad occasionally or on a regular basis. The vast majority of K-Serbs, however, over 85% stated that they do not receive any financial support from family members abroad.

**Table 2: My family member(s) that live abroad support me financially**

| | Ethnicity | | |
| | K-Albanian | K-Serb | Others |
| --- | --- | --- | --- |
| on a regular basis | 30.4% | 1.3% | 14.9% |
| occasionally | 51.5% | 12.3% | 41.8% |
| never | 16.2% | 85.1% | 40.3% |

| | | | |
|---|---|---|---|
| DK/NA | 1.9% | 1.3% | 3.0% |
| Total | 100.0% | 100.0% | 100.0% |

Needless to say, the popular belief is that a vast majority of Kosovans want to emigrate and leave Kosova for good. However, the October 2007 poll results show quite the opposite.

**Table 3: According to some data, migration from Kosova is present again. Do you personally plan to emigrate from Kosova?**

*Ethnicity*

| | K-Albanian | K-Serb | Others |
|---|---|---|---|
| Yes | 19.8% | 9.0% | 27.0% |
| No | 75.8% | 82.0% | 70.0% |
| DK/NA | 4.4% | 9.0% | 3.0% |
| Total | 100.0% | 100.0% | 100.0% |

Only 19.8 % of K-Albanians that were interviewed do plan to emigrate from Kosova, while only 9.0% of K-Serbs, and 27.0 % of Other minorities plan to leave. From the current data, we see that the vast majority of Kosovans, regardless of their ethnicity, do not plan to emigrate from Kosova, specifically 75.8% of K-Albanians, 82% of K-Serbs, and 70% of Others do not plan to emigrate from Kosova.

**Table 4: Have you made specific plans to emigrate from Kosova?**

| | *Ethnicity* | |
|---|---|---|
| K-Albanian | K-Serb | Others |

191

|         | K-Albanian | K-Serb | Others |
|---------|-----------|--------|--------|
| Yes     | 41.1%     | 42.9%  | 24.2%  |
| No      | 56.4%     | 46.4%  | 71.0%  |
| DK/NA   | 2.5%      | 10.7%  | 4.8%   |
| Total   | 100.0%    | 100.0% | 100.0% |

It is also important to note that out of those planning to emigrate from Kosova, based on ethnicity, 41.1% of K-Albanians, 42.9% of K-Serbs, and 24.2% of Others, have made specific plans to emigrate. Generally speaking, over 40% of Kosovans who plan to emigrate, have made specific plans about doing so which perhaps indicates that they are very serious about leaving Kosova.

**Table 5: What would be the reason of your emigration?**

|  | Ethnicity | | |
|---|---|---|---|
|  | K-Albanian | K-Serb | Others |
| Unfavourable economic situation in family | 55.2% | 20.0% | 62.9% |
| Joining the family | 4.9% | 8.0% | 9.7% |
| Better economic opportunities abroad | 28.8% | 12.0% | 17.7% |
| Dissatisfaction with the current political situation in Kosova | 3.1% | 52.0% | 4.8% |
| Something else. | 1.8% | | |
| DK/NA | 6.1% | 8.0% | 4.8% |
| Total | 100.0% | 100.0% | 100.0% |

As to why Kosovans want to emigrate, this survey confirms the popular assumption for K-Albanians – who mainly (about 84%) want to emigrate due to the

192

unfavourable economic situation in the family and better economic opportunities abroad. In general, this data is in line with the KHDR 2006 data on reasons for emigration, where over 41% of Kosovans who said they would emigrate, would do so because of economic hardship.[131] About 81% of Other minorities in Kosova would want to emigrate for the same reasons as the K-Albanians, whereas slightly over half of the K-Serbs want to emigrate from Kosova due to dissatisfaction with the current political situation.

**Table 6: According to some data, migration from Kosova is present again. Do you personally plan to emigrate from Kosova?**

|  | Age Group | | | | | |
|  | 18-24 | 25-30 | 31-36 | 37-45 | Older than 46 | Total |
|---|---|---|---|---|---|---|
| Yes | 28.2% | 19.9% | 23.5% | 17.4% | 11.9% | 19.1% |
| No | 65.8% | 74.9% | 70.5% | 77.3% | 84.4% | 75.9% |
| DK/NA | 6.0% | 5.2% | 6.0% | 5.4% | 3.6% | 5.0% |
| Total | 100.0% | 100.0% | 100.0% | 100.0% | 100.0% | 100.0% |

Looking at the different age-groups of those interviewed, it can be seen that as the age of Kosovans increases, their desirability to emigrate decreases. There is one exception in this trend for the age group 25-30 years, whose desirability to emigrate is lower than those in the

[131] Kosova Human Development Report 2006, *Youth – A new generation for a new Kosova*, UNDP Kosova, March 2007

age group 31-36. This might be because this is the average age during which Kosovans usually get married and become family focused (which would normally lower their desire to leave).

As in the case of planning to emigrate by ethnicity, contrary to popular belief only about 25% of Kosovans between the age of 18 and 30 have plans to emigrate, while the vast majority does not.

**Table 7: Have you made specific plans to emigrate from Kosova?**

| | Age Group | | | | | |
| | 18-24 | 25-30 | 31-36 | 37-45 | Older than 46 | Total |
|---|---|---|---|---|---|---|
| Yes | 44.2% | 30.2% | 42.5% | 36.4% | 28.6% | 37.2% |
| No | 50.6% | 67.4% | 57.5% | 63.6% | 61.2% | 58.9% |
| DK/NA | 5.2% | 2.3% | | | 10.2% | 4.0% |
| Total | 100.0% | 100.0% | 100.0% | 100.0% | 100.0% | 100.0% |

Out of those wanting to emigrate, it can be seen that the younger the population, the higher the proportion of those having made specific plans to leave Kosova. The age group of 25-30 again have a lower rate than the 31-36 age group most likely for the reasons noted above. Nevertheless, the data supports the trend that the older the person, the smaller the proportion of those that have made specific plans to leave Kosova.

**Table 8: What would be the reason of your emigration?**

|  | Age Group | | | | | |
|---|---|---|---|---|---|---|
|  | 18-24 | 25-30 | 31-36 | 37-45 | Older than 46 | Total |
| Unfavourable economic situation in family | 51.9% | 64.3% | 57.5% | 51.2% | 45.8% | 53.6% |
| Joining the family | 2.6% | 2.4% | 7.5% | 9.3% | 12.5% | 6.4% |
| Better economic opportunities abroad | 31.2% | 23.8% | 15.0% | 25.6% | 20.8% | 24.4% |
| Dissatisfaction with the current political situation in Kosova | 3.9% | 4.8% | 10.0% | 14.0% | 12.5% | 8.4% |
| Something else. What? | 2.6% |  |  |  | 2.1% | 1.2% |
| DK/NA | 7.8% | 4.8% | 10.0% |  | 6.3% | 6.0% |
| Total | 100.0% | 100.0% | 100.0% | 100.0% | 100.0% | 100.0% |

Once again, an unfavourable economic situation in the family and better economic opportunities abroad, represent the two major reasons as to why Kosovans want to emigrate. More than 70% (on average) of those interviewed in all age groups want to leave Kosova because of these two reasons. The older the population grows, the less significant these reasons for emigration become, except for the age group of 25-30, which slightly breaks the trend for reasons noted above. Interestingly, as age increases, dissatisfaction with the current political situation becomes yet another important reason to leave Kosova (the proportion of people wanting to leave Kosova because of this reason increases as their age group increases, up to the last age group of 46+).

*Publication Details of the 2008 Edition:*

Katalogimi në Botim – (CIP)
*Cataloging in Publication*
Biblioteka Kombëtare dhe Universitare e Kosovës
*The National and University Library of Kosova*

---

338 (496.51)

Bislimi, Faton
   Newborn Kosova: some development and public policy
challenges : a collection of articles about Kosovo's socio-
economic state / Faton Bislimi. – Prishtina : The Victory
University College ; Houston : Jalifat Publishing, 2008. –
169 f.; 21 cm.

Bibliografia pas cdo kapitulli.
*Bibliography presented after each chapter.*

---

Proceeds from this book have been dedicated to the
educational programs of The Bislimi Group Foundation.
Thank you for your support.
**www.bislimi.org**

www.ingramcontent.com/pod-product-compliance
Lightning Source LLC
Chambersburg PA
CBHW030321290526
45785CB00001B/459